FAMILY ORGANIC

Carol Charlton

COOKBOOK

FAMILY ORGANIC

Carol Charlton

Photography by

Mark Williams & Sandra Lousada

COOKBOOK

David & Charles

This book is dedicated to my mother, 'Judy' Charlton

With heartfelt thanks to:

My husband Bryn Jones for his nutritional research and sub-editing and above all for his love, support and encouragement

and

my children Nick and Harriet, their spouses Kate and Dave, and their children Shaska, Max and Beccy for being the 'organic' family

and

all the people who work with us at the Organic Café and Cookshops who are my extended 'organic' family.

A DAVID & CHARLES BOOK

First published in the UK in 2000

A catalogue record for this book is available from the British Library.

ISBN 0 7153 1079 8

Cookery editor: Anne Sheasby
Art editor: Robin Whitecross
Photography by Mark Williams and Sandra Lousada

Printed in Italy by Milanostampa SpA
for David & Charles
Brunel House Newton Abbot Devon

ACKNOWLEDGEMENTS

Thanks to Organic Café chefs, Anne Dorrington, Issa Cissochka and Simon Prest for their help in preparing food for photography and for their daily input into the Organic Café.

Thanks to my commissioning editor Anna Mumford for her enthusiasm and clear thinking; to my publishers David & Charles (especially Susie Hallam, Rebecca Rochester and Jane Trollope); to the book designer and photoshoot entertainer Robin Whitecross; photographers, Sandra Lousada for her imaginative portrayal of family scenes and for capturing the children so beautifully and Mark Williams for once again so skilfully portraying the colours and natural presentation of the food; Anne Sheasby for patiently checking the recipes and Sarah Widdicombe for her thoughtful editing.

The Organic Café is at 25 Lonsdale Road, London NW6 6RA, the Organic Café Cookshops are at 54 Salusbury Road, London NW6, 102 Golborne Road, London W10 and 101 Notting Hill Gate, London W11. All telephone enquiries to 020 7372 1232.

Distributed in the U.S. by
Trafalgar Square, PO Box 257, North Pomfret Vt, 05053
email tsquare@sover.net
www.trafalgarsquarebooks.com

NOTE: Readers in the U.S. should note that additional information about measurement conversions and ingredient equivalents is given on the back flap of the jacket of this book.

Contents

introduction

The organic revolution is here to stay. You can now find organic food in the supermarket, specialist store and street market, but the organic revolution goes deeper than simple availability. It is also about changing the way we think about food.

We are beginning to reject our reliance on convenience over quality which had become so much part of our lives – often because that was all that was available to us. Now good quality organic ingredients are readily available and by taking a little extra time, we can replace the junk food with simple organic food prepared at home to make our families' diets a good deal healthier. Ingredients are at the heart of healthy organic eating and I have provided advice on this in the storecupboard chapter. As a general rule anything that keeps for a long time is not recommended – the fresher you can get your food the better.

But why bother changing traditional ways of shopping and cooking and what exactly is organic food? Organic food is grown without the use of pesticides and herbicides and is not sprayed during or after harvesting. Pesticides are poisons. We still do not know exactly what a cocktail of these chemicals does to us but it is wiser to adopt the precautionary principle – if you can't prove it does you no harm, don't use it! Organic food is farmed in a traditional way without routine administration of antibiotics and yield-increasing hormones. There is a strict monitoring process, so that if you wish you can trace any organic product back to where it began and be sure it has been produced naturally.

Most of us have become far removed from the land on which our food is grown which means that we don't really know how our food is produced – from sowing, growing, harvesting and processing until it reaches our shelves. Healthy food can only grow on healthy land and intensive farming methods must give way to gentler, purer methods. The plain truth is this: food that has been sprayed or injected with chemicals is bad for you.

I first had the idea for this book in 1987, but never got any further. Thirteen years later, I still feel that this book needs to be written, because, although organic food is now widely available and the supermarkets are putting their weight behind the organic movement, we are still, to varying extents, locked in to eating overprocessed, unhealthy food. I still have to battle with my grandchildren on every trip out, with the temptation of additive-ridden sweets, cakes and ices in every corner shop, and a fast food outlet on practically every other street in the world. I hope that this book will help persuade everyone that healthy organic food can be prepared in a trice and provides the basis of a deliciously varied and enjoyable diet.

the storecupboard

Life is much simpler with a list. At the Organic Café we have a 'stock list', which reminds us of all the essential things we need. A list saves money, too, because we only buy the things we know we are going to use or cook. So there are no foolish impulse buys, which then moulder in the storecupboard or fridge while we wonder what to do with them.

You can also take the pain out of shopping if you order by phone and have your groceries delivered to your home. Some companies can deliver virtually everything you need, while you get on with your life. For contact numbers, see the Organic Suppliers section on page 00.

Organic produce costs more than conventional food, but that is because good food costs more to produce than bad food. Growing fruit and vegetables organically requires more labour; animals reared naturally need more space; cold-pressed oils or naturally fermented soya need more care and take more time to produce. This inevitably makes them more expensive – but it also guarantees that they are much better for you. And of course, good health is one of the greatest gifts you can give to your family.

In this first chapter I have talked about both freezing and drying as it makes sense, because organic food tends to be more expensive, to preserve things that are in season. I have also mentioned how important it is to be aware of the chemicals in household products. If you are turning to a healthier way of eating, it makes sense to banish harmful chemicals from your home at the same time.

In the end it is about questioning where things come from, what is in them and how they are produced. If in doubt, remember that there is usually a price to pay in terms of damage to human health or the environment when cheap food and quick fixes are on offer.

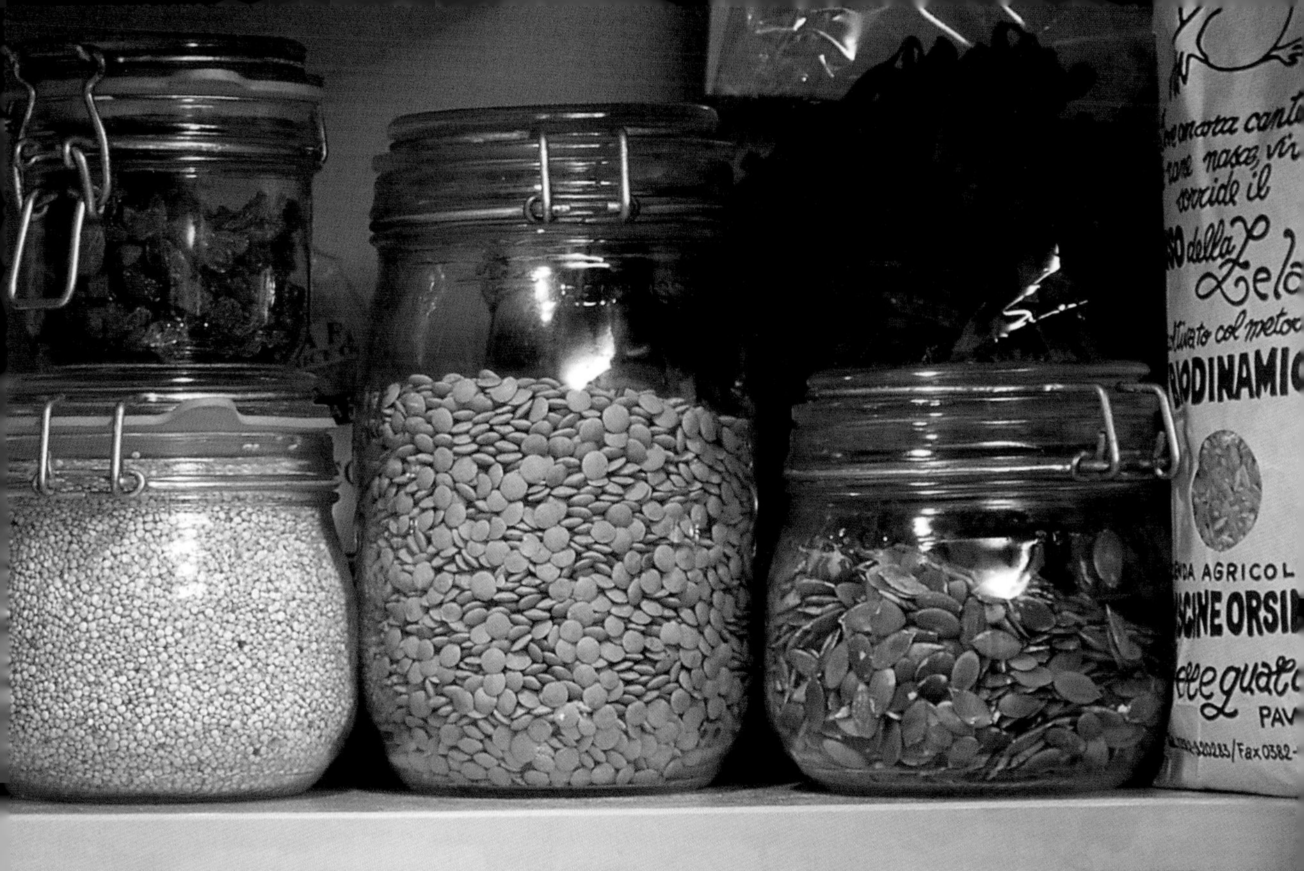
della Zela
ODINAMIC
AGRICOL
SCINE ORSI
PAV

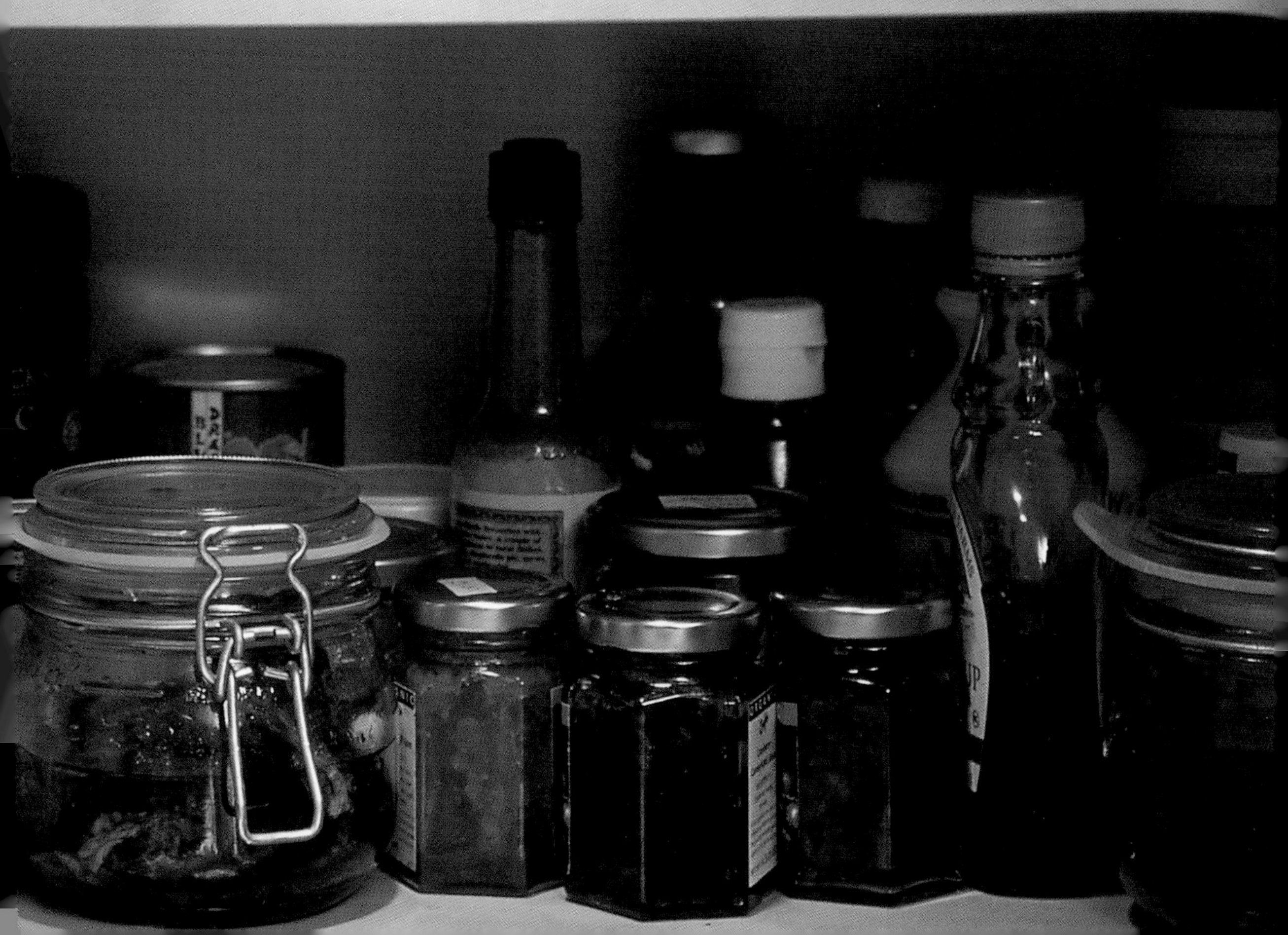

breads

Bread is truly the staff of life and the first and most important basic item on every list. But it must be the right kind of bread: made from organic wholegrain flours. Refined white bread – along with refined white sugar – is the great curse of our age. Stripped of all its goodness by modern steel-milling techniques, bleached white flour is not a healthy option.

So, the first rule for any family is to eat only good organic bread, made from stoneground wholegrains complete with their essential fibre, vitamins and minerals. It doesn't have to be made from wheat. Most countries also have regional breads made from barley, rye and oats, or a mixture of these grains and wheat. So be adventurous in your choice of breads – you will be rewarded with a delicious taste experience.

fats and oils

I am delighted to say that the myth of the fat-free diet has been exploded. We need fat in our diet, but it must be the right kind of fat. There are good fats and bad fats – and what the latest nutritional research tells us is that good fats can protect us from heart disease, strokes, cancers and many other degenerative diseases.

Indeed, without them the body does not function properly: it needs fat to help absorb nutrients. Research now shows that it is better to have tomato sauce that includes olive oil than a fat-free tomato sauce, and that it is better to eat one slice of toast spread with olive oil or butter than two slices of dry toast.

These conclusions came from research into why people living in the Mediterranean region were so much healthier and longer lived than the wealthier northern Europeans and North

Americans. The answer, not surprisingly, turned out to be their diet. These people ate a lot more fresh fruit and vegetables, wholegrains and fish, but what was most interesting of all was that they ate lots of fat – in the form of olive oil, an extremely 'good' fat. In fact, nearly 40 per cent of their calories came from oil.

In northern Europe and North America, a typical diet is high in animal fats such as milk, butter and cheese, and these have their place in a healthy diet, when they are organic and eaten in moderation. The enemy is to be found in the so-called 'hydrogenated' fats found in margarine and the vegetable shortening that is hidden in a wide variety of processed foods. Research shows that these hydrogenated fats lead to high incidences of heart disease and are seriously 'bad' fats, so read the label.

Apart from olive oil, there is another kind of fat in the Mediterranean diet that's good for us: the oil found in cold-water fish like sardines, salmon, herring and mackerel. These fats are good for the blood, preventing clotting and keeping the blood flowing smoothly through the arteries – which is precisely the service they provide for the fish, of course, to keep their blood flowing in icy ocean waters.

So, try to eat fish regularly – say three times a week – if you can. But for those who dislike fish, there are excellent vegetable-based sources of the same fat, such as hempseed, flaxseed (or linseed), rapeseed (or canola) and walnut oils. To achieve a balance of good fats, therefore, you should use all these oils, plus sunflower seed and olive oils. All should be organic and cold-pressed – heating damages the oils and they lose their health-giving properties – and they should be stored in a cool, dark place.

It really is important to distinguish between virgin oils and processed commercial oils, because the latter have undergone mechanical and chemical refining processes such as heating to high temperatures, solvent extraction, bleaching, chemical deodorizing and the addition of preservatives. Many vitamins and minerals are removed in the process.

Of all the oils, hempseed, closely followed by flaxseed, has the best nutritional balance and these two should be eaten raw (you cannot cook with them), but they are very concentrated and so should be used sparingly. My husband likes to dress a tomato salad with organic hempseed oil, lemon juice, sea salt and freshly ground black pepper, but he drizzles the oil over the tomatoes like a miser and mops up the juices with a chunk of good wholemeal bread.

MAKING SEASONED OILS

You can make your own seasoned olive oils to speed up your cooking. I always keep a garlic oil and a chilli oil handy, so that I don't have to crush garlic or chop chillies – the oil already has the flavour. To make your own seasoned olive oils, simply place 2–3 peeled cloves of garlic or 2–3 fresh or dried whole red chillies in the bottom of a pourer bottle and cover with olive oil (about 500ml/18fl oz). Use as required. The longer the oil containing the garlic or chillies is left to stand, the stronger the flavour of the seasoned oil will be.

fruit and vegetables

For optimum health, we should ideally eat 7 servings of fruit and vegetables a day. For many people, this seems an enormous amount and would indeed entail radical shifts of lifestyle. But these servings can be introduced by eating more fresh fruit snacks – and when you know that a serving is a tablespoonful, you will see that you can easily eat 4–5 servings at a meal.

Encourage your family to experiment with the juicer and blender to make weird and wonderful drinks. Encourage them, too, to make home-made lollies with freshly squeezed fruit juices. And remember – an organic apple a day really does help keep the doctor away!

Another good way to eat fruit is by drying it, either in the air or in the oven. It's a great way to preserve fruit and make easy-to-carry snacks – a must for the school lunchbox.

DRYING FRUIT AND VEGETABLES

Stone fruits, such as plums or greengages, can be dried whole or cut in half, in a very cool oven for about 6–8 hours. Apples are best peeled, cored and sliced into rings about 5mm (¼in) thick and soaked in a solution of 55g (2oz) salt to 4.5 litres (8 pints) water for 5 minutes, then drained, patted dry and spread out on trays to dry in the same way as stone fruits. Pears should be peeled, cored and cut into halves or quarters, then soaked in the same saline solution and dried in the same way as apples.

Home-dried vegetables will need about 12 hours' soaking before use. Soak and cook them in the same water, bring to the boil and simmer until they are tender, then drain and serve.

TOMATOES

These dry wonderfully in the oven. Wipe the tomatoes and cut them in half. Place them cut side up on a wire mesh rack (the sort used for cooling cakes) and place this on a baking tray. Sprinkle with coarse sea salt, chopped fresh thyme – add rosemary, too, if you like and a drizzle of olive oil.

Set the oven at 110°C/225°F/Gas Mark ¼ and, leaving the oven door slightly open to allow the humidity to escape during the drying process, place the tomatoes in the oven and leave for about 8 hours (overnight is good, as long as you don't forget that they are in there!). The tomatoes should be dry, but not dried out, and slightly chewy but still soft.

BEANS

Green beans should be prepared as if you were eating them fresh and then blanched in a pan of boiling, slightly salted water for 3–5 minutes. Drain and plunge them into cold water, then drain again and spread out to dry.

MUSHROOMS

Choose very fresh mushrooms – any kind you like – and peel them, then slice if they are very big. String the slices with knots in between them and hang to dry at a temperature not exceeding 50°C/120°F – so not in the airing cupboard!

nuts

And what about nuts? Stick to organic nuts, which will not have been sprayed with post-harvest preservatives to prolong their shelf life. Use them mixed with dried fruit for snacks or in sauces. Walnuts are incredibly high in 'good' fat and make a delicious pasta sauce (see recipe on page 71). Be careful, though, as nuts spoil rapidly when shelled, so store them in a covered container in the fridge.

Warning: Nuts are an excellent source of proteins, vitamins and minerals, but about 1 in every 200 children now has a nut allergy. Avoid giving nuts to under 5s, and test with just a small amount the first time round.

seasonings

SALT

Salt has always been a prized commodity in human history – the word 'salary' is derived from the Latin word for salt, *sal*, which indicates its commercial importance historically. Salting was the main method of preserving foods in the past and still provides us with many delicious dishes, such as salt cod and anchovies.

Today we generally eat far too much salt for our own good – the acceptable daily limit is 5g (⅛oz) per day, but as an example the UK national average is 10–12g (¼oz) per day! This is because the modern Western diet delivers excessive amounts of salt hidden as an additive in processed foods. If you read the labels, you will see that salt has been used in the preparation of almost everything you buy, especially items like canned soup, crisps and nuts, and even biscuits and breakfast foods. In your own cooking, reduce the amount of salt you use and instead add fresh or dried herbs such as oregano, thyme, rosemary, bay, sage, mint or marjoram to enhance the flavour.

Some salt, of course, is essential – both for flavour and for health. Avoid commercial table salts, however, to which chemicals have been added to ensure that they are free running. Instead, buy the various sea salts – some with added marine herbs and plants – which are made by drying sea water in coastal pans exposed to the sun and wind. Sea salt is not purified and so contains many other mineral elements such as iodine, sulphur and phosphorus in trace amounts. So, stick to sea salt, and the less refined the better. For different salt tastes, grind sesame seeds together with coarse sea salt to make the Japanese *gomasio* and store in an airtight jar, or add finely chopped dried seaweeds to coarse sea salt and use as a flavouring.

HERBS

Use fresh organic herbs where possible – or why not grow your own to use fresh or home dried? If you don't have a garden, grow herbs in pots on your windowsills.

DRYING YOUR OWN HERBS

Fresh herbs are best picked on a dry day shortly before they come into flower; for most, this will be early to midsummer. Wash them and pick off and discard any damaged leaves. Dry the herbs by hanging them in the sun or by placing them on a flat tin, baking tray or similar container in a cool oven or airing cupboard. Parsley and mint will stay green if dipped in boiling water for a minute and then dried fairly quickly. Crumble and store the dried herbs in jars in a cool, dark place.

SOYA SAUCE

Soya sauce is a wonderful seasoning, but ensure that it is naturally fermented and made from organic soya beans, as most non-organic soya is made from genetically modified beans. Check that it is labelled either shoyu or tamari. These traditional soya sauces are made from water, whole soya beans and sea salt (plus wheat in the case of shoyu). They contain no preservatives and are unhurriedly aged in wooden casks at natural temperatures for about 2 years.

Unfortunately, nowadays less than 1 per cent of all Japanese soya sauce is made using traditional ingredients and methods. In fact, the soya sauce that we indiscriminately sprinkle on everything is usually the product of a 1-day chemical process and is made with soya extract, ethyl alcohol, sugar, salt, food colouring and preservatives!

SPICES

Always buy spices in small quantities as they will lose their punch very quickly once opened. It is better to buy whole spices and grind them with a pestle and mortar as you need them.

QUICK STOCKS

If you use instant stock – which, let's face it, all of us do when we're in a hurry – organic bouillon powder is now available and should be one of your storecupboard essentials.

QUICK VEGETABLE STOCK

Keep the water in which you have boiled your vegetables to use as stock. Take the vegetables out and fast boil the stock to reduce it down to a concentrated liquid, then cool and freeze this in clean, sterilised milk cartons (fastened with paper clips!). Freeze for up to 1 month.

QUICK FISH STOCK

Make a quick fish stock by boiling 450g (1lb) fresh (scrubbed) mussels in their shells with a glass of white wine (about 175ml/6fl oz wine) for about 5 minutes, then strain and use immediately or cool and freeze. Freeze for up to 1 month.

preserves, sauces and dressings

Sugar and salt are the universal additives in processed and commercial foods that we should most avoid, despite the fact that we usually think of additives as complex E numbers – nasty chemicals whose nature and effects on our health we don't properly understand – not sugar and salt.

Refined sugar – along with refined white flour – poses one of the great health problems of our age. On average, we each eat more than 45kg (100lb) of sugar every year, which is at least 10 times more than our ancestors did, and the results can be seen in the dental decay, obesity and other signs of physical degeneration which are almost universal in our society.

Most of this sugar is consumed in prepared products, such as cakes, biscuits, puddings and ice creams, as well as sauces and dressings. Indeed, it is almost impossible to find a single product on a conventional bakery or supermarket shelf that is not laden with unhealthy sugar, refined flour and hydrogenated fats.

Try making your own jams, sauces, ketchups and dressings – which will contain sugar to be sure, but not refined white sugar with all the goodness stripped out. Instead use unrefined sugar, honey or black treacle, all of which contain more nutrients than refined white sugar.

SALAD CREAM

Heat 125ml (4fl oz) cider vinegar in a saucepan over a gentle heat and gradually whisk in 1 tablespoon plain flour, 1 tablespoon unrefined sugar and ½ tablespoon mustard powder with a pinch of salt. Beat 2 eggs and whisk into the mixture. Remove the pan from the heat and set aside to cool. When cool, whisk in 175ml (6fl oz) double cream and a squeeze of lemon juice until smooth and well mixed. Cover and store in the refrigerator for up to 2 days.

FRENCH DRESSING OR VINAIGRETTE

For my basic oil and vinegar dressing, I do the following: in a glass pourer bottle which holds about 300ml (½ pint) liquid, I place 2 peeled cloves of garlic cut in half horizontally, 1 teaspoon wholegrain mustard, 1 teaspoon sugar and 1 teaspoon vegetable bouillon powder. I then add two-thirds olive oil to one-third cider vinegar, leaving room for 1 tablespoon balsamic vinegar and ½ tablespoon walnut oil. Keep the dressing in your storecupboard and shake before use.

TOMATO KETCHUP

To make about 600ml (1 pint) ketchup, in a jug mix together ¼ teaspoon each freshly ground coriander, cinnamon, cloves, mustard powder (if you want a plain ketchup, leave these spices out) and sea salt, with 1 tablespoon tomato purée and 1 clove of crushed garlic. Add 225g (8oz) sugar and 175ml (6fl oz) cider vinegar. Pour into a saucepan, add three 400g (14oz) cans chopped tomatoes, mix well, then bring to the boil. Simmer, uncovered, for about 40 minutes, stirring occasionally, then cool slightly and purée in a blender or food processor until smooth. If the ketchup is too thin for your liking, thicken it by re-boiling with a little Kuzu (see page 16) or brown rice flour. Set aside to cool and serve cold. Store in a covered container in the refrigerator for up to 2 weeks.

thickening and gelling agents

The BSE issue drew attention to the ingredients to be found in gelling and thickening agents, as many commercial brands of gelatine are made from cattle bones or hides and pigskin, while thickeners are usually made with genetically modified soya products – you will not find this information on the label. Both of these items are used in jams, jellies, yoghurts, confectionery, biscuits, breakfast cereals, bread, cakes and biscuits. The only way to avoid these things is to 'go organic'.

Natural alternatives include an apple pectin extract for jams, called Certo, and Gelozone, a vegetarian alternative to gelatine made from seaweed. Organic maize flour and wild mountain root starch, called Kuzu, can be used to thicken soups, stews, fruit fillings and glazes. Brown rice flour and potato flour are also excellent thickeners, and the latter is gluten-free.

meat, fish and eggs

Organic standards ensure that fish and animals used for meat are reared as humanely as possible, without the use of harmful chemicals. Conventional farming of animals is intensive and the result of these overcrowded conditions is the routine use of antibiotics and growth hormones.

The feed given to intensively farmed animals often contains genetically modified soya – it can make up 20 per cent of a chicken's diet, for example. So, make sure that not only your chicken but also your eggs are organic. What chickens eat comes out in their eggs! Don't risk it – pay more for organic and be sure that your meat and eggs are healthy.

Fish suppliers are a problem. Toxic dumping at sea means that there is no guarantee of healthy fish, while overfishing with gigantic nets not only depletes the fish stocks but also scoops up dolphins and other wildlife. Only one fishing ground is certified organic – St Helena's in the mid-Atlantic – and fish from there is scarce and expensive.

Non-organic fish farms – like all other intensive farming systems – require the routine use of chemicals to kill off the parasites which breed on the overcrowded fish. The number of organic fish farms is steadily increasing, but in the meantime I buy fish which has been caught on the high seas and then frozen or canned within hours. It is best to avoid tinned salmon which will be from non-organic fish farms, and tuna because the dolphins swim with them and are often caught up in the fishing nets.

tofu

Soya bean curd or tofu was once considered to be the staple of vegetarians, but now soya is being hailed as the health food for all of us for the next millennium. (Claims that drinking 3 glasses of soya milk a day can reduce the risk of heart disease by a quarter in just 1 month are just one result of recent research.) Please ensure that your soya is organic, however, as much soya is already genetically modified. Only organic soya will give you a non-GM guarantee.

dairy products

Always choose organic milk, butter, cheese and other dairy products, to avoid pesticide residues and also BST (Bovine Somatotropin), a genetically engineered hormone fed to the cows to increase their milk yield.

Many people are allergic to cow's milk these days. The reason for this isn't entirely clear, but we do know that goat's, sheep's and, for vegans, soya milk are very healthy alternatives – providing they are organic. If they are not, the chances of them containing hormones or being genetically modified is very high, so take note.

If your child cannot tolerate cow's milk, it is a good idea not only to change or organic soya milk but to alternate it with a home-made nut milk made by blending nuts, such as brazils and almonds, or seeds, like sunflower and pumpkin, with water. You will get a liquid that resembles milk, packed with vitamins and minerals.

the freezer

Freezing is a good idea for many reasons. By freezing food when it is really fresh you will retain more vitamins than if you leave it hanging around for a few days. It also allows you to make large batches of things – which hardly takes any longer to do than small batches – and keep them for when you have no time to cook.

It is important to label all food with the contents and freezing date. Ideally, you can put a 'use by' date on as well, but since foods have varying tolerances to freezing, I try to cycle everything over 2 months. However, foods such as berries, for instance, can be kept frozen for up to 1 year. A good investment is a specialist freezer book, which will give you details of the recommended freezing times.

Blanch and dry vegetables before freezing, and freeze them on the coldest temperature possible. When frozen, return the temperature of the freezer to normal.

FREEZER JAM

This is a wonderful method of preserving the taste of fresh soft fruit in the simplest way. These quantities make about 375g (13oz) of jam.

Place 225g (8oz) prepared fresh fruit (such as strawberries, raspberries, blackberries, blueberries, redcurrants, blackcurrants) in a bowl and crush the ripe berries thoroughly using a potato masher or fork.

Layer the crushed fruit and 375g (13oz) sugar together in a bowl, making a total of 4 layers, and leave to stand for 10 minutes. Stir in 2 tablespoons lemon juice and some liquid fruit pectin (see manufacturer's instructions for quantity guide: approximately 1 pouch to 225g/8oz fruit) and continue to stir for about 3 minutes, until most of the sugar has dissolved – a few crystals will remain.

Pour into sterilised jam jars, leaving a 5mm (¼in) space at the top of each jar to allow for expansion during freezing. Cover and leave the jars to stand at room temperature until the jam is set – this could take up to 24 hours.

You can store this jam in the freezer for up to 1 year. It will keep in the refrigerator, covered, for up to 3 weeks. Defrost the frozen jam at room temperature (allow about 1 hour for the jam to soften), then store in the refrigerator.

other essentials

As well as organic unbleached white flour, (plain and self-raising), keep a bag of stoneground wholemeal flour handy and use some of this in your recipes instead of white flour. Try using brown rice flour instead of wheat flour for things like pancakes. Keep a stock of organic dried pastas, too. There are some wonderful ones on the market, ranging from chilli and myrtleberry tagliatelle to wholewheat macaroni.

Personally, I find it hard to change to wholewheat pasta, as for me the taste of good organic white durum wheat pasta is an important part of the pleasure of the meal, and any missing fibre can be supplied in the sauce or the accompanying salads and vegetables. However, if you can introduce your children to wholewheat pasta at an early age, you will be doing them a grand favour.

Organic wholegrains such as brown rice, whole rolled oats, buckwheat, cracked or bulgar wheat, barley (excellent in soups) and couscous should be used as the basis for a wide variety of healthy and tasty meals, in place of polished white rice. Beans and pulses of all kinds are also good storecupboard essentials as they contain valuable amounts of fibre, protein and starch.

a healthy organic home

While we may change our diet to a pesticide-free organic one, we still need to look at the other chemicals in our homes. Pesticides are

present not only in our food but also in household products such as fly sprays. Other dangers lurk, too, in highly perfumed sprays and liquids, that lovely lemony smell in your washing-up liquid, cream cleaner or air freshener blocks is *not* a natural lemon smell. Natural and often organic alternatives are available, so consult your local health food store or even surf the internet. And I suggest that you always keep a bottle of tea tree oil handy as an effective natural disinfectant for your kitchen and bathroom surfaces. You need to be as vigilant about reading the labels on all the products you use in the home as you are about reading the labels on food.

We have to learn to be less wasteful, too. With 6 billion of us now on the planet, where will we be if we continue to cut down trees instead of recycling, or destroy the rain forests to raise cattle for the big burger chains? Meanwhile, we are running out of landfill sites in which to dump our rubbish, even though much of it could be recycled and used as a valuable raw materials.

All your vegetable peelings and garden waste can be composted to feed the soil in your garden. Newspapers and cardboard provide good material for the compost heap, too, if you tear it into smallish pieces and wet it. Even cooked waste can be safely composted in a secure 'wormery'. The rest of your food-associated waste, such as glass and cans, should be recycled by your local council.

And finally, what of microwaves? Personally, I think it is better to be safe than sorry and I always apply the 'precautionary' principle – if you can't prove it does you no harm, don't use it. Recently, the Russians have set their own strict guidelines for microwave safety, concluding that Western safety standards are simply not strict enough. Industry advice to customers is to stay at least an arm's length away from an operating microwave oven, not to operate an oven when it is empty or if the door will not close properly, and never to tamper with the safety interlock or the fuse. After reading that, my advice is not to use a microwave in the first place!

breakfasts and brunches

Breakfast is the most important meal of the day. For many people in today's busy world it is their only chance to eat something wholesome and nutritious until the evening meal. Eating breakfast makes us more alert and less accident prone in the mornings. If there is no time for a proper breakfast, make a 'smoothie' from Chapter 6, to provide a nourishing start to the day. At the weekends, a 'brunch' is the perfect way to catch up with your family and to make plans for the week ahead.

The healthiest breakfast of all is built around fruit, which gives you natural sugars for energy, fibre, vitamins, minerals, antioxidants and other important nutrients. Serve a variety of fruits with the basic breakfast cereals in this chapter for a hearty and healthy first meal of the day.

Breakfast is no time to be thinking about fancy breads, nor is there time for yeasty doughs to rise, so I have included recipes for yeast-free breads and fast breakfast batters. At the weekends you will probably have time to prepare a more leisurely meal, such as breakfast classics like kedgeree and kippers as well as old favourites like Eggs Benedict and Eggs Florentine, which are perfect for celebration days and occasional treats.

On the whole, here, I have aimed to provide a good range of quick, uncomplicated recipes that will give you time really to enjoy your food. While it is tempting to grab breakfast on the run, do try to find time to lay a table and sit down with your family. At least you'll find out what time everyone will be home at night! (If you have children to dress and organise, believe me, I know how nearly impossible this is – my own daughter often ate her porridge on the way to school.)

If you haven't got time to make your own cereals, do buy organic natural cereals with low sugar and salt content. Use organic wholegrain bread for toast and buy organic natural yoghurts and other dairy products.

cereals

In the past we used to incorporate a wide variety of grains in our diet, but nowadays we rely primarily on wheat and tend to ignore the others.

I urge you to try rye, oats and barley, together with lesser-known varieties, as they make a delicious addition to the cereal bowl. Make sure, too, that you eat your cereals in their whole form, not as white bread, white flour and other refined grains which have had the all-important fibre removed, as well as the protein-rich germ and many of the vitamins and minerals as well.

PORRIDGE

In Scotland, porridge is made with water, but I find this a bit spartan. Instead, I use full-fat organic milk, which is much richer or, if I can get it, raw unpasteurized milk, which is just delicious. Add a little salt to bring out the flavour of the oats. You can make a more festive porridge by adding fresh berries in the summer or a dried fruit compote and nuts in the winter. Regard porridge as a valuable nutritional base for a good breakfast and make it part of your weekly diet.

SERVES 4

600ml (1 pint) milk
225g (8oz) rolled oats
2 tablespoons single cream (optional)
a pinch of salt or to taste (optional)

Pour the milk into a heavy-based saucepan and heat gently until boiling. Slowly pour in the oats, stirring continuously with a wooden spoon. Turn the heat right down, so that the porridge hardly appears to be cooking and cook for a further 10 minutes, stirring occasionally. Stir in the cream, if using, and salt to taste.

Serve immediately with milk and maple syrup, honey or blackstrap molasses – a terrific source of vitamin B.

CRUNCHY GRANOLA

Nothing you can buy tastes quite like home-made granola or – with this combination of seeds – will be anywhere near as good for you.

SERVES 4

280g (10oz) rolled oats
55g (2oz) sunflower seeds
55g (2oz) sesame seeds
25g (1oz) pumpkin seeds
175g (6oz) mixed nuts
3 tablespoons clear honey
1 tablespoon canola oil (rapeseed oil) or sunflower oil
1 tablespoon sunflower oil

Preheat the oven to 180°C/350°F/Gas Mark 4. Place the oats and seeds in a bowl and set aside. Chop the nuts roughly, add them to the oat mixture and stir to mix.

Heat the honey and oils together in a small saucepan until the mixture is liquid enough to pour, stirring occasionally. Stir the honey and oil into the oat mixture, mixing well.

Tip the mixture into a shallow, oblong baking tin and bake in the oven for about 20 minutes, or until toasted to a light golden brown colour, stirring once or twice.

Remove from the oven and leave to cool in the baking tin. Once cool, eat immediately or store in an airtight container. Serve with milk, soya milk, yoghurt, fromage frais or fruit juice.

HOME-MADE MUESLI

Mixing cereals with fruit and milk is an old European tradition, but muesli as we know it today was invented by Dr Bircher-Benner, the famous Swiss nutritionist, who used it as a basic dietary cure for many ailments.

Opposite: Creamy porridge with organic maple syrup – sold to the whole family!

SERVES 4

115g (4oz) rolled oats
115g (4oz) rye flakes
115g (4oz) wheat flakes
115g (4oz) barley flakes
115g (4oz) chopped mixed nuts
55g (2oz) sesame seeds
25g (1oz) linseed (or flaxseed)
55g (2oz) raisins or sultanas
grated apple or pear, to serve (optional)

Preheat the oven to 180°C/350°F/Gas Mark 4. Place the oats, flakes, nuts and seeds in a large roasting tin and stir to mix. Bake in the oven for about 20 minutes, or until the nuts are lightly toasted, stirring once or twice.

Remove from the oven and set aside to cool, then stir in the raisins or sultanas. Once cool, eat immediately or store in an airtight container. Add grated apple or pear to serve, if liked, and serve with milk, fruit juice or yoghurt.

breads and batters

For quick breakfast breads and buns, try recipes using baking powder or bicarbonate of soda to do the same job as yeast. By buying unbleached, wholegrain, stoneground flours and breads, you will ensure a healthy breakfast base.

SIMPLE SODA BREAD

In Ireland, soda bread is traditionally made with unpasteurized buttermilk. If you can't find this, a good alternative is to use a mixture of sour cream and water.

MAKES 1 LOAF

450g (1lb) plain wholemeal flour
2 teaspoons salt
1 teaspoon bicarbonate of soda
175ml (6fl oz) sour cream

Preheat the oven to 220°C/425°F/Gas Mark 7. Lightly grease a baking sheet and set aside. Place the flour, salt and bicarbonate of soda in a large bowl and stir to mix.

Whisk the sour cream and 175ml (6fl oz) water together, then gradually stir it into the flour mixture. Knead lightly, then shape into a ball and place on the prepared baking sheet.

Take a long knife and cut halfway through the loaf one way, then do the same the other way, so that the loaf is in four equal sections.

Bake in the oven for about 30 minutes, covering the top of the loaf with greaseproof paper towards the end of the cooking time if it starts to brown too much. Remove from the oven and cool on a wire rack for about 15 minutes before cutting and serving.

CORN BREAD

This is a bread made with batter and you can add ingredients to give it a different twist. For instance, here you could add thinly sliced onions, finely shredded hot chillies, or my favourite – a handful of crisply fried bacon pieces.

SERVES 4

115g (4oz) plain flour
115g (4oz) maize meal
3 teaspoons baking powder (must be a level teaspoon)
1 teaspoon salt
225ml (8fl oz) milk or half milk and half natural yoghurt
1 egg
2 tablespoons runny honey
3 tablespoons butter, melted
115g (4oz) fresh, frozen (defrosted) or canned (drained) sweetcorn kernels

Preheat the oven to 200°C/400°F/Gas Mark 6. Lightly grease a shallow 20cm (8in) square or 23cm (9in) round

Opposite: This Corn Bread is crammed with juicy kernels

baking tin and set aside. Place the flour, maize meal, baking powder and salt in a large bowl and stir to mix.

Beat the milk or milk and yoghurt, egg, honey and melted butter together and stir in the sweetcorn kernels (and bacon or other flavouring, if using). Add this mixture to the dry ingredients and mix well to make a batter.

Pour the mixture into the prepared baking tin and spread it out evenly. Bake in the oven for about 25 minutes or until cooked and golden – the bread should spring back when lightly pressed. Turn out onto a wire rack and cool slightly, then cut and serve while still hot.

BREAKFAST PUFF BUNS

These are light and airy, crisp and puffy – very like Yorkshire puddings - with a custardy lining. They are delicious served straight from the oven with jam and butter, or with scrambled eggs.

MAKES 12

- 55g (2oz) butter, melted, plus extra for brushing
- 115g (4oz) self-raising flour
- ½ teaspoon salt
- 4 eggs, beaten
- 225ml (8fl oz) milk

Preheat the oven to 190°C/375°F/Gas Mark 5. Brush a 12-hole muffin tin with melted butter, both inside the holes and on the top of the tin. Preheat the prepared tin in the oven while you make the batter. Place the flour and salt in a bowl, then add the eggs and melted butter and beat until evenly mixed.

Add the milk and beat the ingredients together until smooth and well mixed. Pour the batter into the preheated muffin tins, filling each muffin hole about two-thirds full.

Bake in the oven for about 35 minutes without opening the oven door, until risen, golden and crisp, then remove from the oven, turn out and serve immediately.

CORN FRITTERS

I love these little fritters, full of plump and juicy sweetcorn kernels. The addition of the lime leaves gives them an aromatic flavour which I find quite addictive. Serve them with bacon and eggs or simply as a snack.

MAKES ABOUT 20

- 115g (4oz) frozen (defrosted) or canned (drained) sweetcorn kernels
- 115g (4oz) maize meal
- a pinch of salt
- 2 eggs, beaten
- 175ml (6fl oz) milk
- 4 fresh or frozen lime leaves, finely chopped
- sunflower oil, for frying

Coarsely chop the sweetcorn kernels in a food processor or by hand, then set aside. Place the maize meal in a bowl with the salt, add the eggs and half the milk and beat until smooth. Beat in the remaining milk, then fold in the chopped sweetcorn and lime leaves. Taste and add more salt if necessary.

Heat about 2.5cm (1in) oil in a wok and test to see if it is hot enough by dropping in a tiny bit of the corn batter – it should sizzle immediately. When the oil is hot enough, cook the fritters in batches – drop dessertspoonfuls of the corn batter into the hot oil and fry for about 5 minutes, or until crisp and golden, turning the fritters once to ensure they are golden all over.

Remove and drain on absorbent kitchen paper, then place on a plate and keep warm while cooking the remaining fritters. Serve warm.

Opposite: Breakfast Puff Buns. Serve these 'puffballs' of batter straight from the oven as they are collapsing

BUCKWHEAT BLINIS

The traditional recipe calls for a yeast sponge, but for a quicker version we use self-raising flour.

MAKES ABOUT 24 SMALL OR 12 LARGE BLINIS

- 140g (5oz) self-raising flour
- 85g (3oz) buckwheat flour
- ½ teaspoon salt
- 425ml (¾ pint) milk
- 3 large eggs, separated
- 2 tablespoons butter, melted

Sift the flours and salt into a large mixing bowl. Make a well in the centre and pour in half the milk, bringing the flour to the centre with a wooden spoon and gradually combining it with the milk. Add the egg yolks and remaining milk and whisk to make a smooth batter – this can be done by hand or in the food processor.

Stir in the melted butter, then just before you are ready to cook the blinis, whisk the egg whites in a separate bowl until quite stiff and fold them into the batter.

Cook the blinis in batches, 3 or 4 at a time, either on a lightly buttered hot griddle or in a large non-stick frying pan over a moderately high heat. Drop spoonfuls of the batter onto the griddle or into the frying pan, or use a small mould to pour or spoon the batter into if you find this easier – ideally they should be no more than (5–7.5cm (2–3in) in diameter and about 5mm (¼in) thick. Cook the blinis on each side until golden, turning once, then remove, place on a plate and keep warm while you finish cooking the remaining blinis.

If you are feeling extravagant, you can serve the blinis with smoked salmon or with caviar and sour cream. For 12 breakfast blinis, you will need about 225g (8oz) smoked salmon or caviar and 300ml (½ pint) of sour cream.

Below: These Brecon Light Cakes simply fly out of the pan and onto our breakfast table when the grandchildren visit for the weekend

BRECON LIGHT CAKES

These are the Welsh version of griddle scones, and are made from a batter flavoured with orange juice and served with brown sugar. As with all pancakes, you can substitute maple syrup for the sugar. If you have a wheat or gluten allergy, try substituting brown rice flour for the self-raising flour.

MAKES ABOUT 12

- 2 eggs
- 2 tablespoons freshly squeezed orange juice
- 115g (4oz) self-raising flour, or brown rice flour

½ teaspoon salt
55g (2oz) sugar
3 tablespoons milk
25g (1oz) butter
1 tablespoon brown sugar or maple syrup

Place the eggs and half the orange juice in a bowl and beat them together until they are well mixed. Next, sift the flour and salt into a separate bowl and then stir in the sugar. Pour in the egg mixture and stir well, then mix in the milk to form a fairly thick, smooth batter. Melt the butter in a heavy-based frying pan over a medium heat and when it begins to sizzle, drop tablespoonfuls of the batter into the pan, allowing about 5cm (2in) between each of the cakes.

Cook the cakes on each side until golden brown, turning once, then remove and drain on absorbent kitchen paper. Place on a plate and keep warm, while cooking the remaining cakes. Serve warm, sprinkled with brown sugar or maple syrup and the remaining orange juice.

eggs

Eggs make a wonderful breakfast – but not when served too often with bacon or sausages, because the 'saturated' fat in the pork and bacon is not only bad for your family's hearts, but also for their waistlines! This great traditional English breakfast should be served as an occasional treat, not as a standard item in the diet.

Eggs on their own, however, are a much healthier option as we need the vitamins and minerals they contain.

By choosing organic eggs, you know they were laid by hens that lead natural lives in the open air and feed on natural foods. Healthy hens lay healthy eggs, so it's worth paying a little extra for eggs you can trust, and we all know the consequences of feeding farm animals with unnatural foods.

By the way, nutritional experts say four eggs a week is about the maximum for good health, so enjoy your eggs but don't eat them everyday.

EGGS AND BACON

For that special treat, nothing beats the classic dish of eggs and bacon. Make sure it is special by choosing the best ingredients, by which I mean organic bacon from healthy, free-range pigs, as well as organic eggs. Non-organic bacon is pumped up with water and bathed in chemical preservatives (no wonder it doesn't taste very nice!) while the smoked version is unlikely to have been naturally smoked – the 'smoke flavour' has probably been added as a liquid solution.

OMELETTES

The omelette is a much-discussed item: some people like them flat, others like them so fluffy that they beat the whites separately, as with a soufflé omelette. For one person, use 1–2 eggs, seasoning and a sprinkling of chopped fresh herbs, plus a knob of butter for cooking.

Here are a few pointers to ensure the perfect omelette. Invest in an 18cm (7in) omelette pan with a heavy base so that the heat is transferred evenly. This can be non-stick or not. If not, just heat a tablespoon of salt in the pan and rub well into the surface with absorbent kitchen paper. Tip the salt away and wipe the pan with a clean cloth.

Heat the pan before you make your omelette, then quickly whisk the eggs together with the seasoning and any herbs you may be using. Melt the butter in the pan over a medium heat and pour the omelette mix into the hot butter. Draw the egg mixture back from the edges of the pan using a palette knife, allowing any liquid egg to run into the space this creates. Stop doing this when the eggs are set and cook the egg mixture for another minute – the omelette should move freely when you shake the pan.

Tilt the pan slightly and, using the palette knife, fold the omelette in half, taking care not to break it. It should look creamy inside and golden on top. Turn the omelette onto a warm plate and serve immediately.

If you are filling the omelette, make sure the filling is hot and place it on one half of the omelette in the pan before you fold the other half over the filling. You can put anything in an omelette or simply mix chopped fresh herbs into the egg mixture. Try filling your omelettes with fruit as a change from pancakes – especially if you are following a wheat-free diet.

SOUFFLÉ OMELETTE

Soufflé omelettes are often served with sweet fillings or simply dredged with icing sugar.

Allow 2 eggs per person. Separate the egg yolks and whites, then, in a bowl, whisk the whites with 1 teaspoon sugar until stiff. In a separate bowl, whisk the yolks together with 2 tablespoons water until creamy. Melt a knob of butter in the pan, then gently fold the yolk mixture and the whites together with a spatula and pour into the pan.

Cook over a medium heat until golden brown underneath and firm to the touch, then place under a preheated hot grill until set – this will take only a matter of minutes. Gently run the spatula through the middle of the omelette and fold it over. Slide the omelette onto a warm plate and dredge with sifted icing sugar. To be swanky, heat a skewer over a live flame and mark a criss-cross on the top of the omelette.

CHOCOLATE SOUFFLÉ OMELETTE

For a weekend brunch special, try this chocolate soufflé omelette. Simply melt 25g (1oz) organic chocolate and allow it to cool. Add the melted chocolate to the beaten egg yolks with 1 tablespoon milk (this replaces the 2 tablespoons water used in the recipe above), then fold in the whisked egg whites. Cook as above.

WHITE OMELETTE

This alternative white omelette is ideal for people who are trying to eat less cholesterol – which is, of course, found in the yolk of the egg. The yolkless omelette is a very acceptable alternative because, while being light and fluffy, it is still substantial enough to satisfy a hungry breakfast appetite.

Simply separate the yolks and the whites – use 2 whites per omelette and omit the sugar used in the soufflé version. Beat the whites until they form peaks and cook as above for a standard omelette. Use the yolks for another recipe.

OMELETTE SUZETTE

Follow the recipe above for Soufflé Omelette, allowing 2 eggs per person and using 1 tablespoon Grand Marnier mixed with 1 tablespoon water in place of the 2 tablespoons water used for the Soufflé Omelette. Then, when the cooked omelette is served on a warm dish, pour a further 2 tablespoons of the warmed liqueur around the omelette, light it up and serve!

Above: Rich, dark organic chocolate is melted into this soufflé omlette mixture

Above: The richness of creamy Hollandaise Sauce combined with egg yolk is cut by the earthy taste of spinach in Eggs Florentine

EGGS FLORENTINE AND EGGS BENEDICT

The basis for both of these dishes, apart from eggs, is that delicious concoction – hollandaise sauce. Thanks to the food processor, making hollandaise sauce need not be such a difficult, long-drawn-out operation. I keep trying to bring our chefs at the Organic Café round to the benefits of modern kitchen appliances, but they will not be turned from the classic method.

Typically, these egg dishes are served on muffins, but you can use toast or rolls cut in half, if you prefer. Don't forget: when you are using organic spinach and other vegetables, you do need to wash them thoroughly under running water. No pesticides means that caterpillars and slugs may still be lurking!

HOLLANDAISE SAUCE

SERVES 4

3 large egg yolks
salt and freshly ground black pepper
1 tablespoon lemon juice
1 tablespoon white wine or cider vinegar
175g (6oz) butter

Place the egg yolks in a blender or food processor with salt and pepper and blend for about 1 minute. Heat the lemon juice and vinegar in a small saucepan until just coming to the boil, then switch the blender or processor on again and pour the hot liquid into the egg yolk mixture in a slow, steady stream. Switch off the blender or processor.

Using the same saucepan, gently melt the butter in the pan taking care not to let it brown, then, once again, switch the blender or processor on and pour in the butter in a slow trickle.

Turn the blender or processor off and scrape the sides of the bowl with a spatula. Switch on again for a brief burst and you should now have a lovely, smooth classic hollandaise sauce. Use as required for Eggs Florentine or Eggs Benedict.

EGGS FLORENTINE

SERVES 4

225g (8oz) fresh spinach leaves or frozen spinach, defrosted and squeezed to extract all the moisture
4 eggs
about 1 tablespoon white wine vinegar, for poaching the eggs
4 muffins, toasted, or 4 slices of your favourite bread, toasted
butter, for spreading
1 quantity Hollandaise Sauce (see recipe above)
freshly ground black pepper (optional)

Cook the thoroughly washed fresh spinach leaves in a small amount of boiling water in a large covered pan or wok for a few minutes until tender – I find a wok is useful for fast cooking vegetables in the minimum amount of water. Drain the spinach thoroughly and squeeze out any excess moisture. If the leaves are large, roughly chop them. Alternatively, sauté the frozen (defrosted) spinach in a pan without water for a few minutes, then squeeze out any excess moisture.

Meanwhile, soft poach the eggs in a saucepan of fast-boiling water to which you have added a little white wine vinegar. Do this by breaking each egg into a large metal spoon and lowering it into the water. Cook for about 2–3 minutes or until the yolk has whitened over, then lift the egg out of the pan with a slotted spoon and drain.

Spread the hot muffins or slices of toast with butter, top with the cooked spinach followed by the poached eggs, then spoon the hollandaise sauce over the top. Finish with freshly ground black if liked pepper and serve.

Above: The sublime taste of ham and eggs together is topped by this sumptuous Hollandaise Sauce to make Eggs Benedict

EGGS BENEDICT

SERVES 4

For this recipe, you will need about 225g (8oz) cooked honey-roast ham or grilled back bacon rashers. Follow the same process as above for Eggs Florentine, but instead of using spinach, place a slice or two of ham or a rasher or two of grilled bacon on the toasted buttered muffins or slices of toast and place the poached eggs on top. Spoon the hollandaise sauce over this, season with black pepper if liked and serve.

Even teenagers can enjoy making their own butter!

yoghurt, butter and cream

Amazingly, about 70 per cent of all the people in the world cannot digest milk or dairy products because their bodies lack a special enzyme. They can eat yoghurt, however, because it comes already digested – the bacterial cultures in live yoghurt do the job of the missing enzyme in the human body.

Yoghurt has many proven health benefits, helping to boost our natural defences against colds, virus infections and possibly even tumours. And, because it comes pre-digested, the calcium content is easily taken up by the body, to help build strong bones and teeth.

Yoghurt is truly universal – where animals give milk, people make yoghurt. Its beneficial properties are thought to help the Georgians in the Caucasian mountains of southern Russia to live the long and healthy lives for which they are renowned.

There is a delicious selection of organic yoghurts in the shops today, both plain and fruit, Greek-style and standard, but it is fun to make your own and children really enjoy it. It gives them a sense of how food changes and which food comes from what source.

The most beneficial yoghurt is the one you make yourself.

HOME-MADE BUTTER

You need several children for this operation as it is hard work to keep shaking, so it's a good school holiday project. You will also need full-fat organic milk.

Pour 1.2–1.7 litres (2–3 pints) milk into a screw-top jar and churn the butter by shaking the jar – this should take about 20 minutes. When the butter and milk separate, you will be left with buttermilk (excellent served on muesli, for example) and butter. Drain off the buttermilk and place the butter in a dish, cover and store it in the refrigerator.

HOME-MADE YOGHURT

Yoghurt can be made in a vacuum flask or in a covered glass container or glass pots left in a warm place (such as an airing cupboard) to set.

Take 600ml (1 pint) full-fat milk to make 600ml (1 pint) yoghurt. Pour 1 tablespoon of the milk into a bowl and mix with 1 teaspoon live natural yoghurt. Set aside. Gently heat the remaining milk in a saucepan until it is fairly hot, but not boiling – you should be able to hold your finger in it for several seconds.
Stir the reserved milk and yoghurt mixture into the hot milk, then pour the milk into a vacuum flask or other container(s) and replace the lid or cover to seal. Leave the yoghurt to set – the 'vacuum flask method' will take about 6 hours and the 'airing cupboard method' overnight. In these days of central heating, the kitchen overnight will be probably be sufficiently warm. Once made, store the yoghurt in a covered bowl or jug in the refrigerator. Serve with seasonal fresh fruit or Dried Fruit Compôte (see recipe on page 156). For extra nourishment and flavour, add sesame and pumpkin seeds.

HOME-MADE CRÈME FRAÎCHE

Take the same weight or volume of double cream and sour cream and whisk them together in a bowl. Cover with a clean cloth and allow the mixture to stand in a warm kitchen or other warm spot overnight, or until thickened. In the cold weather this could take as long as 24 hours. Once thickened, serve or store in a covered bowl in the refrigerator. Use sparingly, as this is a rich concoction – a dollop on porridge with a drizzle of maple syrup is a Sunday special!

smoked fish

smoked fish has always been a popular British breakfast food, with names such as smelts, kippers, smokies and bloaters conjuring up the formal breakfast tables and silver chafing dishes of Victorian homes.

Smoking is the traditional method of preserving fish, but beware: choose only naturally smoked fish, as many manufacturers use chemical flavourings to imitate the smoky taste and give the fish its yellow colour. Look for mail-order smokers, as these are usually small companies which produce fine hand-crafted products. The degree of the smoking determines the length of time the fish will keep – this is why some smoked fish can be eaten uncooked and others which have only been lightly smoked should be poached or grilled before eating.

Smoked haddock is terrifically versatile and no brunch section would be complete without its inclusion. As with smoked cod, the fillets of these fish are usually taken from large fish and may be coarse-textured. Smokies are haddock or whiting with their heads cut off, which have been hot-smoked. Bloaters and bucklings are versions of smoked herring, as are kippers, which are lightly brined and smoke-cured over wood chips. Kippers are usually served poached or grilled.

JUGGING KIPPERS

For the traditional method of cooking kippers, place the fish in a jug and cover them with boiling water, then leave in a warm place for 5–10 minutes. Lift out, drain and serve with a knob of butter on top.

KEDGEREE

My own preference for kedgeree is brown rice, which is certainly not traditional, but I think the nutty flavour improves to the overall taste and anyway, it's better for you!

SERVES 4-6

6 cloves
6 cardamom pods, lightly crushed
1 teaspoon cumin powder
about 700ml (1¼ pints) fish stock or bouillon powder dissolved in boiling water
½ teaspoon saffron threads or turmeric
2 bay leaves
700g (1lb 9oz) smoked haddock fillet (try to buy a thick fillet if you can)
350g (12oz) long grain white or brown rice
115g (4oz) butter
1 teaspoon curry powder
3 eggs, hardboiled, shelled and chopped
125ml (4fl oz) single cream
salt and freshly ground black pepper
1 tablespoon finely chopped fresh parsley

Place the cloves, cardamom and cumin in a wide, heavy-based saucepan and dry-fry them until they start to release their fragrance, stirring occasionally. Add the fish stock or bouillon powder dissolved in boiling water, the saffron or turmeric and the bay leaves.

Add the fish, cover and poach gently for about 8 minutes or until just cooked. Remove the fish from the pan using a fish slice, place it on a plate, cover and set aside.

Add the rice to the pan and bring to the boil. Reduce the heat, cover and simmer for about 15 minutes if using white rice and for about 40 minutes if using brown rice, or until the rice is cooked and all the liquid is absorbed, stirring occasionally. Add more stock, if required.

If you are serving this to children, don't forget to take out the cloves, cardamom pods and bay leaves before serving. Adults can do it themselves!

Opposite: Kedgeree made with brown rice lends a different, nutty texture to a breakfast classic. Garnish with a sprinkling of boiled egg yolk for a special occasion

Remove the pan from the heat, take off the lid, then leave the rice covered with a tea towel to absorb the steam. Remove and discard the skin and any bones from the fish and roughly flake the flesh.

Melt the butter in a heavy-based sauté pan, stir in the curry powder, then add the flaked fish. Cook for about 30 seconds, then stir in the cooked rice and chopped eggs. Using a slotted fish slice, toss the mixture over a medium heat for about 2 minutes, or until it is hot.

Stir in the cream and continue to heat and toss the mixture for 3–5 minutes, or until hot. Season to taste with salt and pepper, then pile the kedgeree onto warmed serving plates. Sprinkle with chopped parsley and serve.

If you want to make this more of a lunch dish, add lightly cooked vegetables such as green beans or broccoli florets to the kedgeree before serving.

BAKED SMOKED FISH CREAMS

This golden, creamy haddock dish has its origins on the coast of Scotland and is traditionally made with Finnan haddock (or haddie, as the Scots call it). If you dare, serve it with triangles of bread fried in butter, or perhaps melba toasts for a healthy alternative.

SERVES 4

450g (1lb) skinless smoked haddock fillets
freshly ground black pepper
4 eggs
300ml (½ pint) single cream
½ teaspoon turmeric

Preheat the oven to 180°C/350°F/Gas Mark 4. Cut the fish fillets into small pieces and place in the bottom of four greased individual ramekins (about 7.5cm/3in in diameter) or one 1.2 litre (2 pint) pie dish, then season well with black pepper.

Whisk the eggs, cream and turmeric together in a bowl, then pour over the fish. Cover the ramekins or pie dish with buttered greaseproof paper and place in a large baking tin filled with 2.5cm (1in) cold water.

Cook in the oven for about 40 minutes or until browned and set. Serve hot with fried bread or buttered toast.

SMOKED FISHCAKES

This is an easy fishcake recipe – perfect for breakfast. Make the fishcakes with smoked haddock or smoked cod, and add smoked salmon if you want a really special dish.

SERVES 4

450g (1lb) potatoes, diced
25g (1oz) butter
225g (8oz) skinless smoked haddock or smoked cod fillets
300ml (½ pint) milk or half milk and half water
1 tablespoon finely chopped fresh parsley
salt and freshly ground black pepper
1 egg, beaten
fresh breadcrumbs, for coating
olive oil or sunflower oil, for cooking

Cook the potatoes in a saucepan of boiling water for 10–15 minutes or until tender. Drain thoroughly, then mash them with the butter (I would probably use more butter, but then I was trained in France!).

Meanwhile, place the fish in a frying pan and add the milk or milk and water. Bring to a simmer, then cover the pan and poach the fish for about 5 minutes or until just cooked. Remove the fish from the milk using a slotted spoon, place it on a plate and leave to cool slightly.

Flake the fish, then add the fish and parsley to the mashed potatoes and mix well. Season to taste with salt and pepper and bind with a little of the milk in which the fish was cooked, if necessary. Discard the remaining milk.

Using your hands, form the mixture into 8 round, flat cakes. Dip the cakes in the beaten egg and coat all over with breadcrumbs, patting them on well to make them stick.

Heat a little oil in a large frying pan and fry the fishcakes over a medium heat for about 3 minutes on each side, or until crisp and golden, turning once. Drain well on absorbent kitchen paper, then serve with home-made Tomato Ketchup (see recipe on page 15) or with Fast Fresh Tomato Sauce (see recipe on page 102).

SMOKED FISH PLATTER

Simply arrange a selection of smoked trout, eel and salmon on a platter with a little fresh watercress. Serve with a horseradish cream made either by mixing bought horseradish sauce with a little cream or crème fraîche, or by making the real thing following the recipe below.

HORSERADISH CREAM SAUCE

This recipe is from Marcel Boulestin, who opened the first true French restaurant in London in 1925 and wrote numerous cookery books and newspaper columns. His advice to his readers was to 'taste a grain of rice, prick the meat, feel it with the finger, eat a fried potato, and you will then know if it is ready or not. No absolutes, only compromises'.

If you grate your own horesradish, beware, the fumes will get in your eyes and up your nose, so stand well back!

'Put in a small saucepan a tablespoonful of vinegar and two chopped shallots. Reduce by half, add finely grated horseradish and a small cup of cream. Bring to the boil and let simmer for a quarter of an hour, at the end of which the sauce has thickened properly. It should be quite thick. It can be passed through a strainer or not, according to taste, and served hot or cold.'

snacks and lunches

Beware of processed commercial snacks! Most of them are packed with sugar, salt, saturated fats, food colourings, chemical flavourings and other nasties. And they are nearly always made with refined carbohydrates – white flour and white rice – and then cooked in cheap, frequently rancid, oils.

Everyone needs refuelling fast at some point or another. You may be stuck on the train having missed breakfast or in too much of a rush to eat a proper lunch. Children and pregnant women, in particular, need constant refuelling, and a mid-morning or mid-afternoon snack revives flagging energies for everyone.

Despite their bad name, snacks can also be good wholesome food, so don't pack your children's school lunchboxes with artificially flavoured crisps and other processed snacks. There are delicious alternatives, as you will discover in this chapter.

Plan ahead when you travel and don't leave yourself at the mercy of fast-food outlets when you're on a train or in a car. Fat-laden burgers, fries and sweet fizzy drinks are the fastest way to put on excess weight and destroy teeth and bones. Instead, make your own food and have a healthy, happy picnic. It tastes better – and it's a lot cheaper, too!

Of course, with children you won't be able to avoid all junk foods. My grand-daughter Shaska gets so tired of being lectured about eating healthy organic food that she sometimes says 'I'd like an ice-cream please, but not organic!' At that moment, her mother and I recognize overkill in our health message. But still I say, be strong and stand firm: it's your family's health we are talking about here, and snack foods are the number one enemy.

Of course, we all need to buy food on the move from time to time, but when this happens look first for packets of organic dried fruit and nuts and organic fruit and for sandwiches with fresh fillings. Check other snacks for additives and high levels of sugar and salt. Above all avoid fried things or burgers where the meat content is zilch and the nasties many.

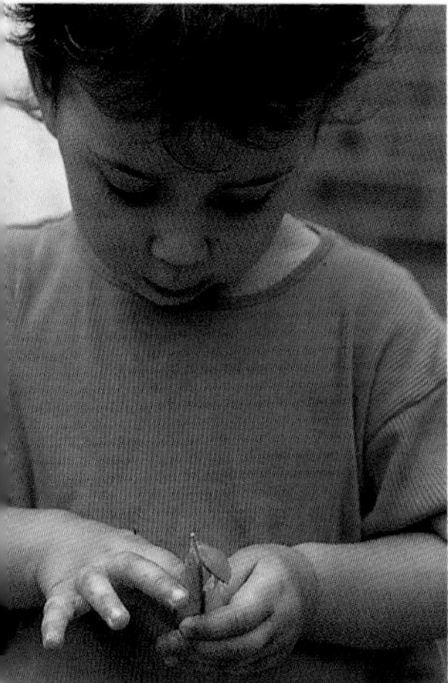

Above and below: Encourage children to become involved in preparing vegetables and, who knows, their curiosity may get the better of them! Below right: Tamari and Sesame Carrots

enjoy your greens!

Most children are wary of vegetables and while there is little point in fighting it head on, you shouldn't give up either.

There are definitely some vegetables that are more popular than others – so keep trying different ones until you find some successes. It helps if you don't offer children choices in the first place. Plan your meals and serve them with the expectation that they will be eaten – and keep those vegetables on the menu!

There are also ways of preparing vegetables so that they will be more palatable for children. Make dips for raw carrots, serve cold cooked French beans with vinaigrette, try tossing carrots in tamari and sesame seeds (see panel right), add cheese sauce to the cauliflower and serve vegetables with tomato sauce. For more entrenched refuseniks, try thinking laterally: tomato sauce, carrot cake and pumpkin pie are good ways of convincing children that vegetables aren't all that bad!

It helps too if you involve children in growing and cooking vegetables and herbs. Children love to have their own little plot or windowbox to tend, and if they grow something edible they are more likely to give it a try themselves. Encourage them to cook outside. Once your children are boy scout and girl guide age, show them how to make a small fire or give them a little Japanese barbecue that sits on the ground (always under your supervision, of course). They could brew up their own cowboy meal of baked beans.

TAMARI AND SESAME CARROTS

Peel the carrots, then cut them in half widthways (or into three if they are large) and then into quarters, lengthways, so that you have a bundle of long, thin carrot batons.

Heat a little olive oil in a wok, add the carrots and stir-fry for 3-4 minutes. Add a small handful of sesame seeds and 2 teaspoons tamari and toss for a further 1-2 minutes. Serve hot.

VARIATIONS

You can make this recipe with leftover broccoli stalks instead. Stir-fry crushed garlic with the broccoli and finish with a squeeze of lemon juice.

Another alternative is to toss cooked hot carrots with butter, chopped fresh basil, a touch of maple syrup and a pinch of salt.

Above: The fresher the better with sweetcorn as it loses its sweetness the longer it is stored.
Left: Dips to eat with either raw or cooked, cold vegetables are popular with all ages. French beans prove to be much more palatable when coated with yoghurt dip (see page 44).
Below: There's no need to peel organic carrots, just wash them

dips and pâtés

A great way to eat raw vegetables is to provide a tasty dip. Try to choose a vegetable of every colour for your raw vegetable platter – as a general rule of thumb, this will give you a complete spectrum of vitamins.

You can also use these dips for the Sesame Crackers or Sour Cream Chilli Crackers (see recipes on page 46), or simply spread them on organic wholemeal toast and eat with salad for a highly nutritious meal.

The following dips serve between 4 and 6 people.

WALNUT AND CREAM CHEESE DIP

115g (4oz) cream cheese
115g (4oz) Greek yoghurt
225g (8oz) chopped walnuts
1 tablespoon olive oil
1 teaspoon paprika
pinch of cayenne pepper
1 clove garlic, peeled and chopped
1 tablespoon chopped fresh herbs, such as chives or parsley

Simply place all the ingredients in a blender or food processor and blend until smooth or mix by hand for a crunchy version using a pestle and mortar to break the nuts down if they are too big. Spoon into a dish and serve immediately, or cover and chill in the refrigerator before serving.

YOGHURT AND FETA DIP

Savoury yoghurt dips can be made with a variety of seasonings, such as balsamic vinegar or soya sauce. Use Greek yoghurt, or thicken plain yoghurt with some crème fraîche, or mix with feta cheese as here. You could add chopped cucumber for extra crunch.

175g (6oz) feta cheese
3 cloves garlic, crushed
3 tablespoons olive oil
1 tablespoon lemon juice
2 tablespoons chopped fresh mint
175g (6oz) Greek yoghurt

Place the feta cheese in a bowl and mash with a fork. Add the garlic, oil, lemon juice, mint and yoghurt and mix well. Cover and chill in the refrigerator until ready to serve.

CRUNCHY NUT DIP

Simple crunchy dips can be made by oven-roasting nuts and seeds and blending them together.

115g (4oz) hazelnuts
115g (4oz) sesame seeds
olive oil, to drizzle
salt, to taste

Preheat the oven to 200°C/400°F/Gas Mark 6. Spread out the hazelnuts and sesame seeds on separate baking sheets. Drizzle over a little oil, then roast in the oven for about 5 minutes for the sesame seeds and about 10 minutes for the hazelnuts or until lightly browned.

Place the roasted nuts and seeds in a blender or food processor with a pinch of salt and blend until roughly smooth and well mixed. If the mixture is too dry, add a further few drops of olive oil and blend to mix. Spoon into a dish and serve.

TARAMASALATA

I don't anyone know who does not like this cod's roe pâté. My husband has it for breakfast, my children and their children eat it straight out of the bowl with a finger!

1 thick slice of white bread, crusts removed
225g (8oz) smoked cod's roe
2 cloves garlic, crushed
salt and freshly ground black pepper
300ml (½ pint) olive oil
juice of ½ lemon

Place the bread in a bowl, cover with cold water and leave to soak for about 10 minutes. Squeeze the bread until it is almost dry and discard the water. Crumble the bread into a bowl or blender or food processor.

Remove and discard any unwanted lumps from the cod's roe, then add it to the bread with the garlic and black pepper. Stir to mix then beat or blend to form a thick paste.

Gradually add the oil (just as you would if you were making mayonnaise), about 1 teaspoon at a time, beating or blending continuously, until all the oil has been added – you will end up with a thick, creamy, pale pink paste.

Beat or blend in the lemon juice and add a little more black pepper to taste. The mixture should be salty enough, but add a little salt to taste, if necessary.

Spoon into a dish, cover and chill in the refrigerator until ready to serve.

AUBERGINE PÂTÉ

For vegetarians, this is an alternative to taramasalata. It has that delicious smoky, lemony flavour and the same sort of texture.

2 medium aubergines
115g (4oz) tahini
1 onion, minced
3 cloves garlic, crushed
juice of 1 lemon
1 tablespoon finely chopped fresh parsley
salt and freshly ground black pepper
1 tablespoon olive oil

Preheat the oven to 200°C/400°F/Gas Mark 6, then reduce the temperature to 180°C/350°F/Gas Mark 4 just before you put the aubergines in the oven. Cut the stems off the aubergines, prick them all over with a fork and place them directly on the oven shelf. Roast in the oven for about 45 minutes or until totally soft and baggy.

Remove the aubergines from the oven wearing oven gloves, then set them aside to cool. Once cool, scoop out the insides of the aubergines into a bowl or blender or food processor. Add all the remaining ingredients except the olive oil and mash together thoroughly or blend until well mixed.

Spoon into a dish, cover and chill in the refrigerator for at least 30 minutes before serving. Drizzle the olive oil over the top of the pâté just before serving.

SMOKED FISH PÂTÉ

This recipe is so easy – simply buy a pack of smoked fish, like mackerel, trout or salmon (you can now find organically-farmed smoked trout and salmon, see page 16) and off you go. Invest in a pair of tweezers and it will take you 5 minutes max.

225g (8oz) smoked trout
115g (4oz) cream cheese
juice of ½ lemon
150ml (¼ pint) natural yoghurt
salt and freshly ground black pepper

Remove and discard all the skin and bones from the mackerel. Place the mackerel in a blender or food processor with the cream cheese and lemon juice and blend until you have a purée. Alternatively, mash the fish in a bowl, then beat in the cream cheese and lemon juice until mixed together – this will make a rougher pâté.

Add the yoghurt and blend or mix well, then season to taste with salt and pepper. Spoon into a dish, cover and chill in the refrigerator for at least 30 minutes before serving.

savoury snacks

Savoury nibbles, crisps and biscuits are increasingly part of our fast-food lifestyle, but they need not be shop bought. If you make your own using organic ingredients you can provide healthy food to bridge the gap between meals.

SOUR CREAM CHILLI CRACKERS

You can add more chilli to this recipe or take it out altogether, according to your taste and your 'customers'!

MAKES ABOUT 48

175g (6oz) plain flour
¼ teaspoon baking powder
pinch of salt
55g (2oz) butter, melted
142ml (5fl oz) carton sour cream
1 teaspoon chilli powder

Sift the flour, baking powder and salt into a bowl and make a well in the centre. Mix the melted butter, sour cream and chilli powder together and pour into the well. Using a wooden spoon, slowly introduce the flour from the sides into the centre, stirring continuously, until the mixture forms a soft, slightly sticky dough.

Turn onto a lightly floured surface and knead lightly until smooth. Wrap the dough in a clean cloth and chill in the refrigerator for about 30 minutes.

Preheat the oven to 190°C/375°F/Gas Mark 5. Lightly grease 2 baking sheets and set aside. Roll out the dough on a lightly floured surface to a thickness of about 3mm (⅛in). Cut into rounds using a 5cm (2in) cutter. Place the rounds on the prepared baking sheets and prick each one all over with a fork.

Bake in the oven for about 10 minutes or until golden brown and crisp. Serve immediately or transfer to a wire rack to cool. Store in an airtight container.

SESAME CRACKERS

These tasty little crackers are delicious with dips and spreads or just on their own.

MAKES ABOUT 24

115g (4oz) plain flour
55g (2oz) maize meal
¼ teaspoon salt
¼ teaspoon bicarbonate of soda
1 tablespoon runny honey
25g (1oz) butter, diced
55g (2oz) sesame seeds
1 tablespoon cider vinegar

Preheat the oven to 190°C/375°F/Gas Mark 5. Lightly grease 2 baking sheets and set aside. Place the flour, maize meal, salt and bicarbonate of soda in a bowl and stir to mix. Drizzle in the honey, then lightly rub the butter into the flour mixture using your fingertips, until it resembles coarse breadcrumbs.

Stir in half the sesame seeds, then gradually add the vinegar and 7 teaspoons water, stirring the mixture with your hand until the dough is sticky. Shape the dough into a ball and knead until smooth.

Roll out the dough on a lightly floured surface to a thickness of about 3mm (⅛in). Cut into rounds using a 5cm (2in) cutter. Place the rounds on the prepared baking sheets and prick each one all over with a fork. Sprinkle with the remaining sesame seeds, pressing them in lightly.

Bake in the oven for about 10 minutes or until lightly browned and crisp. Transfer the crackers to a wire rack to cool, then store in an airtight container (if there are any left over!).

Opposite: Sesame Seed Crackers and Sour Cream Chilli Crackers with a selection of spreads

CHEESE AND HERB SNAPS

You don't have to use parmesan cheese for these snaps – and some people dislike the taste – just increase the amount of hard cheese and leave out the parmesan.

MAKES ABOUT 30

- 85g (3oz) cheddar or other hard cheese, finely grated
- 25g (1oz) parmesan cheese, finely grated
- 1 teaspoon finely chopped fresh thyme
- 1 teaspoon finely chopped fresh parsley

Preheat the oven to 200°C/400°F/Gas Mark 6. Line a baking sheet with non-stick baking paper and set aside. Place the cheeses and herbs in a bowl and stir to mix. Place a 5cm (2in) round pastry cutter on the prepared baking sheet and sprinkle about 1 teaspoon of the cheese and herb mixture into the cutter. Remove the cutter and repeat this process, taking care to leave a gap between each snap.

Bake in the oven for about 4–6 minutes or until they are golden and set. Lift the snaps off the baking sheet with a palette knife and transfer to a wire rack to cool. Alternatively, while they are still hot, curl each snap over a round object such as a bottle or a rolling pin – you will have to work fast as they harden very quickly as they lose their heat – then place on a wire rack to cool. Repeat this process until all the cheese and herb mixture has been used up and cooked. Serve cold. Store in an airtight container.

nuts and seeds

Nuts and seeds are highly nutritious and natural snack foods, just as they come. But you can also jazz them up by quickly pan-frying or oven-roasting them in the coating of your choice.

PAN-FRIED SALTED ALMONDS

Simply toss whole almonds – in their skins or out of them – in a wok over a medium heat with a drizzle of olive oil and a sprinkle of salt for a minute or two, until toasted to a light golden colour. Add more salt before serving if you think it necessary. Flakes of sea salt are great for this as they are soft and melt in with the oil. Add an optional pinch of chilli powder if you are serving the almonds with drinks for adults. Store in an airtight container.

OVEN-ROASTED SOYA-COATED NUTS AND SEEDS

Cashew nuts are delicious cooked in this way, but seeds such as sesame, sunflower and pumpkin also roast well and taste great.

Choose good soya sauce – either shoyu or wheat-free tamari (see page 14) – and preheat the oven to 150°C/300°F/Gas Mark 2. Spread out some nuts or seeds on a baking sheet or in a baking tin and bake in the oven until golden – about 20 minutes for nuts and 15 minutes for seeds.

Remove from the oven, sprinkle with soya sauce (taking care not to put too much on) and stir until all the sauce is absorbed – this won't take long and no liquid should remain. Serve hot, or leave to cool and store in an airtight container.

Right and left: Almonds are delicious pan fried. Toss them in a wok with a drizzle of olive oil and a little sea salt

SPICY OVEN NUTS

You should gauge the amount of chilli you use according to who is eating these delicious nuts.

SERVES 6

2 tablespoons olive oil
1 teaspoon salt
1 teaspoon garlic powder
2 teaspoons chilli powder
1 teaspoon ground coriander
1 teaspoon ground ginger
225g (8oz) mixed whole nuts

Preheat the oven to 150°C/300°F/Gas Mark 2. Mix the oil, salt, garlic and ground spices in a bowl. Add the nuts and toss until coated all over with the spicy oil.

Spread out the nuts on a baking sheet or in a roasting tin and cook in the oven for about 30 minutes or until golden, shaking the tin occasionally.

Drain the nuts on absorbent kitchen paper and sprinkle with more salt to taste. Serve immediately, or cool and store in an airtight container for up to 2 days.

To reheat, simply place the spicy nuts in a roasting tin and reheat in a preheated oven at 150°C/300°F/Gas Mark 2 for about 5–10 minutes before serving.

sweet snacks

At the risk of being boring, I say again: think twice before buying sweet snacks. That's not to say never – we all fall for that bar of chocolate or bag of toffees from time to time – but the chances of their containing hidden nasties, like colouring and chemical flavours as well as lots of saturated fat and sugar, are high. Use these delicious home-made alternatives to fend off sugar cravings. As well as being sweet they are also nutritious, so should keep hunger pangs at bay, too.

OATMEAL AND RAISIN COOKIES

Cookies are just oversized biscuits, but their size gives them more substance and texture than conventional biscuits. After making cookies, biscuit-making seems just too fiddly.

MAKES ABOUT 24 COOKIES

175g (6oz) butter, softened
225g (8oz) sugar
1 egg
1 teaspoon vanilla extract
175g (6oz) plain flour
1 teaspoon ground cinnamon
½ teaspoon bicarbonate of soda
½ teaspoon salt
125ml (4fl oz) maple syrup
350g (12oz) rolled oats
140g (5oz) raisins

Preheat the oven to 180°C/350°F/Gas Mark 4. Grease 2 baking sheets and set aside. Cream the butter and sugar together in a bowl, add the egg and beat together to mix. Add the vanilla and 2 tablespoons water and beat to mix.

Sift the flour, cinnamon, bicarbonate of soda and salt into the egg mixture and stir to mix well. Stir in the maple syrup, then add the oats and raisins and mix well.

Drop tablespoonfuls of the mixture onto the prepared baking sheets, then flatten each one with a fork, leaving indentations on the top.

Bake in the oven for about 15 minutes or until golden and firm to the touch. Cool slightly on the baking sheets, then transfer to a wire rack to cool completely. Store in an airtight container.

SPICED MOLASSES COOKIES

MAKES ABOUT 24 COOKIES

175g (6oz) butter, melted
200g (7oz) sugar
90g (3¼oz) molasses or black treacle
1 egg
200g (7oz) plain flour
½ teaspoon ground cloves
½ teaspoon ground cinnamon
½ teaspoon baking powder
½ teaspoon salt

Preheat the oven to 180°C/350°F/Gas Mark 4. Lightly grease 3 baking sheets and set aside. Place the melted butter in a large bowl with the sugar and molasses or black treacle and mix together thoroughly. Lightly beat the egg, then add to the butter mixture and mix together until well blended.

In a separate bowl, sift the flour, ground spices, baking powder and salt together, then add this to the butter mixture. Beat all the ingredients together to make a fairly thick, smooth batter. Drop tablespoonfuls of the mixture onto the prepared baking sheets, leaving a 10cm (4in) gap between them. Bake in the oven for 12–15 minutes or until lightly browned. Remove from the baking sheets while still soft using a palette knife and transfer to a wire rack to cool. Repeat until all the mixture is used up. Store in an airtight container for up to 1 week.

Opposite: Oatmeal and Raisin and Spiced Molasses Cookies

traybakes

Traybakes are quick and easy to make. Simply spoon your mixture into a tin and bake in one large piece. When cool, cut into bars or squares and serve.

FRUIT AND CEREAL BARS

This recipe provides healthy, satisfying snack for lunchboxes and teatime. I have based it on the flapjack recipe we use in the restaurant, in which we substitute black treacle for golden syrup – black treacle or molasses contains lots of important minerals, golden syrup is the liquid equivalent of refined sugar!

MAKES 12 BARS

115g (4oz) plain flour
1 teaspoon bicarbonate of soda
85g (3oz) rolled oats
55g (2oz) sultanas
55g (2oz) ready-to-eat dried apricots, chopped
55g (2oz) desiccated coconut
140g (5oz) butter
115g (4oz) sugar
1 tablespoon molasses or black treacle

Preheat the oven to 180°C/350°F/Gas Mark 4. Grease a 23cm (9in) square or 18x28cm (7x11in) oblong baking tin and set aside. Place the flour, bicarbonate of soda, oats, sultanas, apricots and coconut in a bowl and stir to mix.

Place the butter, sugar and molasses or black treacle in a saucepan and heat gently, stirring, until melted and blended. Pour onto the oat mixture and stir until well mixed. Turn the mixture into the prepared tin and press down evenly.

Bake in the oven for 15–20 minutes, then cool slightly, before cutting into bars. Loosen the edges of the bars, then leave to cool completely in the tin. Remove from the tin and store in an airtight container for up to 1 week.

CARROT CAKE FINGERS

MAKES 12 FINGERS

175g (6oz) carrots, finely grated
finely grated zest and juice of 1 orange
350g (12oz) plain wholemeal flour
2 teaspoons baking powder
1 teaspoon ground cinnamon
½ teaspoon ground allspice
175g (6oz) butter, melted
175g (6oz) sugar
3 eggs
1 teaspoon vanilla extract

Preheat the oven to 150°C/300°F/Gas Mark 2. Grease a 23cm (9in) square or 18x28cm (7x11in) oblong baking tin and set aside. Place the carrots in a bowl, add the orange juice and stir to mix. Set aside.

Sift the flour, baking powder and ground spices into a bowl and set aside. In a separate bowl, beat together the melted butter and sugar until well mixed, then beat in the eggs one at a time. Add the grated orange zest and vanilla extract and beat again until well mixed.

Gradually fold the dry ingredients into the butter mixture, adding some grated carrots and orange juice in between, so that you have some dry ingredients, some carrots and so on, finishing with the flour. Fold all these ingredients together with a light, uplifting movement.

Turn the mixture into the prepared tin and level the surface. Bake in the oven for about 45 minutes or until the cake is cooked and golden brown – when cooked it will spring back at the touch of your finger.

Leave to cool in the tin for 10 minutes before cutting into fingers. Remove from the tin and place on a wire rack to cool. Serve cold. Store in an airtight container.

Opposite: Fruit and Cereal Bars are quick and easy to traybake

school lunchboxes

When I was at school, the midday meal was carefully planned to provide us with a balanced diet. This, combined with the free milk, meant that children had all they needed to get through the day. Nowadays, few secondary schools provide lunch and, even if they do, the children also have the option of eating out of school. Children head for fast food outlets, food that is so robbed of nutritional value and so tricked out with chemical additives that it is steadily reducing their natural resistance to sickness and disease.

Although admittedly not entirely effort-free for parents, a well-prepared lunchbox can easily provide all the nutrients required to see your child through an energetic day at school. If you start them young you will establish good eating habits which will make them less likely to stray later on.

Above: Sunflower seeds roasted the in oven mixed with soya sauce (see recipe on page 48)

WEEKLY MENU

MONDAY

Pasta salad, roasted sunflower seeds, nectarine, carrot cake, apple juice

TUESDAY

Avocado wholemeal sandwich, fresh fruit jelly, Green & Blacks chocolate bar, cherry juice

WEDNESDAY

Pitta Bread stuffed with Greek salad, mixed nuts, yoghurt and honey, banana smoothie

THURSDAY

Beach Bum's rice salad, mixed fruit and nuts, fresh fruit salad, elderflower cordial

FRIDAY

Spanish tortilla, wholemeal bread and smoked fish pâté, cherry tomatoes, apple, sparkling water

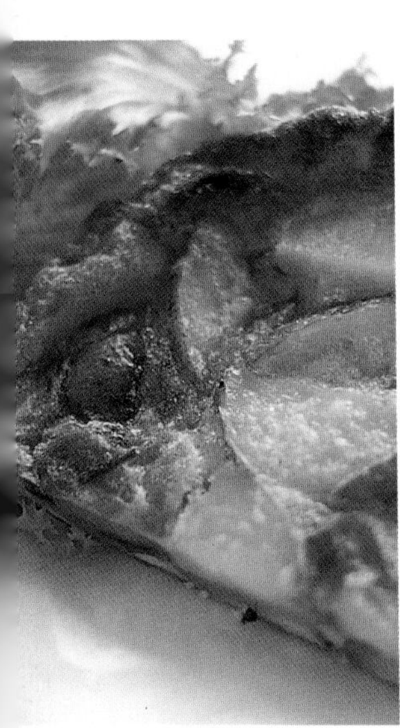

Far left: Spanish tortilla (see recipe on page 138)
Centre: Pitta bread stuffed with Greek salad (see recipe on page 56)
Left: Carrot cake (see recipe on page 52)
Opposite: Inside Thursday's tasty lunchbox with Beach Bum's rice salad (see recipe on page 56), mixed fruit and nuts and fresh fruit salad

Above: pasta salad
Opposite (clockwise from top left): home-made yoghurt with honey and pistachio nuts; healthy wholegrain sandwich with avocado and tomato; fresh fruit juices in handy recycled containers

Sandwiches made with wholegrain bread are proper food, but white 'cotton wool' bread delivers no nutrition – it just fills you up for a short time. Try introducing raw vegetable finger food, like carrot sticks or cherry tomatoes. If you then add a piece of fruit – organic, of course – you will go a long way to keeping your children healthy through rain or shine. For lunchbox desserts mix creamy organic yoghurt with honey and nuts (but not for under 5s, see page 12) for a high protein, calcium boost.

BEACH BUM'S RICE

So-called because we used to take this to the beach with us every summer. Simply sauté chopped onion and garlic in a little olive oil and seasoning until soft, then add in chopped bacon until cooked, or ham, then chopped fresh tomatoes, green beans, frozen peas or corn.

This recipe is great for using up left-overs as you can throw in whatever you've got to hand. Add some cooked rice and mix everything together. Adjust the seasoning and serve warm or cold.

GREEK SALAD

Combine together chopped tomatoes with chopped cucumber, olives and crumbled feta cheese. Toss together with a little vinaigrette dressing (for the dressing see recipe on page 15).

PASTA SALAD

Again cold pasta is mixed with chopped fresh tomatoes, flaked line-fished tuna and chopped parsley, then seasoned and dressed with a little vinaigrette. Virtually anything can be added to pasta to make a lunchbox salad. For an older child with a larger appetite, pack a piece of wholegrain bread to soak up any juices.

FRUIT SALAD

Simply combine any chopped fresh fruit, include sweet juicy favourites such as grapes and peaches, and moisten with a little fruit juice.

FRUIT AND VEGETABLE JUICES

Try to include freshly-sqeezed juices in the lunchboxes, or at least real juice with no added sugar. Otherwise, pack a small bottle of still mineral water – sometimes called 'brain food' because the grey cells require constant watering!

soups as a meal

When I lived in Spain with a young family and not much money, I quickly came to appreciate the hearty soups that the Spanish serve their families. For them, tight budgets mean that meat is served as an accompaniment rather than the main feature.

So, a little belly of pork and some bones are added to chickpea and chard stews, while ham bones are the basis for thick lentil soups. These soups are kept on the hob and continually re-boiled, with the addition of extra vegetables, such as potatoes and carrots.

Although generally regarded as winter fare, soups can also be good for summer lunches and I have provided recipes for several classic chilled soups that are ideal for the hottest days of the year.

SMOKED HADDOCK AND SWEETCORN CHOWDER

This dish is a meal in itself, with a lovely combination of sweet, hot and smoky flavours, held together by the creamy consistency.

SERVES 4

- 25g (1oz) butter
- 1 onion, finely chopped
- 1 small fresh red chilli, deseeded and finely chopped
- 2 medium potatoes, diced
- 200g (7oz) sweetcorn kernels, fresh or canned (drained)
- 1.5 litres (2¾ pints) vegetable stock
- 450g (1lb) skinless boneless natural-smoked haddock fillet
- 225ml (8fl oz) double cream
- 1 tablespoon chopped fresh parsley
- squeeze of lemon juice
- salt and freshly ground black pepper

Melt the butter in a heavy-based saucepan, add the onion and chilli and cook until the onion is turning golden, stirring occasionally. Add the potatoes, half the sweetcorn and the stock and stir to mix. Bring to the boil, cover and simmer for about 15 minutes, or until the potatoes are cooked, stirring occasionally.

Remove the pan from the heat and cool slightly, then purée the soup in a blender or food processor until smooth. Return to the rinsed-out pan, reheat gently, then add the fish, cover and poach the fish in the hot soup for 5–10 minutes or until it is just cooked but still firm, stirring occasionally. Fork the fish into bite-sized pieces.

Stir in the remaining sweetcorn, the cream, parsley, lemon juice and seasoning and reheat gently until piping hot, stirring occasionally. Ladle into soup bowls. Serve.

CALDO VERDE

This is the broth my husband cooks up as an imitation of the Iberian classic – the name literally means 'Green Broth' – when he wants to use all the vegetable cooking water he has been freezing for such a purpose. Ever since he was told by a nutritionist to drink the water he boiled the potatoes in, he squirrels away vegetable water in used, well-washed milk cartons and freezes them. Use spinach or chard for this healthy brew. All the ingredients are simply placed in a pan and simmered until tender – this is definitely a man's dish!

SERVES 4

- 450g (1lb) potatoes, cut into small dice
- 2 cloves garlic, crushed
- 1 large onion, sliced
- 450g (1lb) fresh green leaves such as spinach or chard
- 1.4 litres (2½ pints) vegetable stock (or vegetable bouillon powder dissolved in boiling water)
- salt and freshly ground black pepper

Opposite: This colourful Smoked Haddock and Sweetcorn Chowder is a family favourite

Place all the ingredients in a large saucepan and stir to mix. Bring to the boil, cover and simmer for about 20-30 minutes, or until the vegetables are cooked and tender, stirring occasionally. Adjust the seasoning to taste and ladle into soup bowls to serve.

VEGETABLE SOUP

This is the perfect soup for the organic vegetarian. The wholesome, gutsy flavours of the organic vegetables make a satisfying soup for a winter's day.

SERVES 4

1 tablespoon butter
1 tablespoon olive oil
1 large onion, sliced
1 clove garlic, crushed
2 sticks celery, roughly chopped
1 leek, washed and chopped
5 medium potatoes, diced
1 small squash, such as butternut squash, peeled and diced
1 tablespoon vegetable bouillon powder
2 teaspoons chopped fresh or dried thyme
2 sprigs of fresh tarragon, chopped, or 1 teaspoon dried tarragon
4 leaves of fresh sage, chopped, or ½ teaspoon dried sage
salt and freshly ground black pepper

Heat the butter and oil in a large heavy-based saucepan until the butter has melted. Add the onion, garlic, celery and leek and sauté until the vegetables are turning golden brown, stirring occasionally.

Add the potatoes, squash, bouillon powder, herbs, seasoning and 1.4 litres (2½ pints) water (or enough water to cover the vegetables) and stir to mix.

Bring to the boil, cover and simmer for about 20 minutes or until the vegetables are soft, stirring occasionally. Remove the pan from the heat and cool slightly, then purée the soup in a blender or food processor until smooth. Return to the rinsed-out pan and reheat gently until hot, stirring so that the soup doesn't stick. Ladle into soup bowls and serve.

CHICKPEA, CHICKEN AND CHORIZO SOUP

My sojourn in Spain left me with a love for the humble chickpea. In Italy, they make a soup with chickpeas and pasta, but in Spain they make it with chickpeas and potatoes. Usually *chorizo* sausage will be added (yes, you can even get organic *chorizo* now!) and some pieces of chicken.

SERVES 4

225g (8oz) dried chickpeas
1 tablespoon olive oil
1 large onion, sliced
2 medium leeks, including 5cm (2in) of the green stems, washed and sliced
8 small joints skinless chicken or a whole small skinless chicken cut into 8 small joints (about 1.3–1.8kg/3–4lb in weight)
2 cloves garlic, finely chopped
450g (1lb) medium potatoes, cut into quarters
900g (2lb) cabbage, shredded
2 carrots, sliced
1 bay leaf
4 fresh parsley sprigs
450g (1lb) chorizo or other garlic smoked pork sausage, cut into 2.5cm (1in) chunks
½ teaspoon freshly ground black pepper
salt, to taste

The day before you want to eat the soup, place the chickpeas in a sieve or colander and wash thoroughly under cold running water. Place them in a bowl and cover with about 1.7 litres (3 pints) cold water and leave to soak overnight.

The next day, heat the oil in a large, heavy-based saucepan, add the onion and leeks and cook gently until softened, stirring occasionally. Add the chicken joints and cook until sealed all over, turning occasionally. Add the garlic and 1.4 litres (2½ pints) water. Drain the chickpeas and add to the saucepan. Bring to the boil, then cover and simmer gently for 1½ hours, stirring occasionally.

Add the potatoes, cabbage, carrots, bay leaf, parsley and *chorizo* and stir to mix. Cover and simmer for a further 30 minutes or until the chicken, chickpeas and vegetables are cooked and tender, stirring occasionally. Remove and discard the bay leaf, then season with black pepper and salt to taste. Ladle into large soup bowls and serve.

VICHYSSOISE

This is a classic iced soup, smooth with the consistency of cream. It can be hard to find leeks in the summer, so if you shop using a vegetable box scheme you may need to substitute the leeks with a mild-flavoured onion, such as a Spanish onion. If you really love this soup like I do, you could make the basic soup and freeze it before adding the crème fraîche or cream.

SERVES 4

25g (1oz) butter
3 large leeks, white part only, washed and thinly sliced
1 stick celery, thinly sliced
2 medium potatoes, thinly sliced
1.2 litres (2 pints) chicken or vegetable stock (jellied chicken stock is traditionally used for this soup)
salt and freshly ground black pepper
150ml (¼ pint) single cream or crème fraîche
1 tablespoon snipped fresh chives

Melt the butter in a large saucepan, add the leeks, celery and potatoes and sweat over a gentle heat, until the vegetables are soft but not coloured, stirring occasionally. It is important that the vegetables do not brown as this will spoil the colour of the soup – it is better to undercook them slightly.

Add the stock and seasoning, then bring to the boil, cover and simmer for about 15 minutes, or until the vegetables are cooked and tender, stirring occasionally.

Remove the pan from the heat and cool slightly, then purée the soup in a blender or food processor until smooth. Pour into a bowl, stir in the cream or crème fraîche, then taste and adjust the seasoning. Set aside to cool.

Once cold, whisk for a few seconds, then cover and chill in the refrigerator for at least 2 hours before serving. Ladle into soup bowls to serve and garnish with the snipped chives.

TOMATO AND BASIL SOUP

This simplest of soups is equally good served either hot or cold and is probably the quickest soup you will ever make. New evidence shows that tomatoes contain lycopene, a powerful antioxidant with cancer-fighting properties, so make this a regular part of your diet.

SERVES 4

450g (1lb) tomatoes, roughly chopped
1 onion, chopped
600ml (1 pint) vegetable stock
1 tablespoon tomato purée
1 tablespoon chopped fresh basil
salt and freshly ground black pepper
fresh basil sprigs, to garnish

Place the tomatoes, onion, stock, tomato purée and chopped basil in a blender or food processor and blend until smooth and well mixed. Sieve the soup into a bowl, discarding the contents of the sieve. Season the soup with salt and pepper to taste.

If serving hot, pour the soup into a saucepan and heat gently until piping hot, stirring occasionally. If serving cold, cover and chill in the refrigerator for at least 2 hours before serving. Ladle into soup bowls to serve and garnish with fresh basil sprigs.

CHILLED BEETROOT BORSCHT

You can now buy organic pre-prepared beetroots, which makes this an easy dish to prepare for a hot summer's day. If you are cooking your own beets, save the cooking water to dye any drab white cotton or silk underwear a saucy shade of pink!

SERVES 4

- 450g (1lb) fresh (topped and tailed) or ready-cooked beetroots
- 500ml (18fl oz) vegetable stock (or vegetable bouillon powder dissolved in boiling water)
- 1 medium cucumber, coarsely grated
- 125ml (4fl oz) freshly squeezed orange juice
- 4 spring onions, finely chopped
- 1 tablespoon chopped fresh dill
- salt and freshly ground black pepper
- 225ml (8fl oz) sour cream or crème fraîche
- fresh dill sprigs, to garnish

If using fresh beetroots, peel them, cut into quarters and place them in a saucepan with the stock. Bring to the boil, cover and simmer for about 15 minutes or until cooked. Remove the beetroots from the stock using a slotted spoon, place them on a plate and set aside to cool. Pour the stock into a large bowl and set aside to cool. Coarsely grate the beetroots, add them to the cooled stock and stir to mix.

If you are using ready-cooked beetroots, simply peel and coarsely grate them, add them to the vegetable stock and stir to mix.

Add the cucumber, orange juice, spring onions, chopped dill and seasoning to the beetroot and stir to mix. Cool, then cover and chill in the refrigerator for at least 2 hours or until very cold.

Whisk together the sour cream or crème fraîche and 2 teaspoons cold water, reserve a little for the garnish, then add the rest to the soup. Stir to mix, then taste and adjust the seasoning. Ladle into soup bowls to serve and top with a spoonful of sour cream or crème fraîche. Garnish with dill sprigs.

KING PRAWNS IN THAI BROTH

This soup looks wonderful and is just a simple, tasty broth full of succulent prawns. You can, if you like, omit the oil and butter and simply boil the leeks and ginger in the stock until soft, then add in the prawns and simmer until cooked. Season, and throw in the coriander just before serving. This recipe would also make a good main course, if served with cooked rice.

SERVES 4

- 1 tablespoon butter
- 1 tablespoon olive oil
- 2 leeks, washed and chopped or thinly sliced
- 1 teaspoon peeled and grated fresh root ginger
- 24 raw peeled king prawns
- 1.2 litres (2 pints) vegetable stock
- 2 stalks of lemon grass, peeled and bruised
- salt and freshly ground black pepper
- 1 tablespoon finely chopped fresh coriander

Heat the butter and oil in a heavy-based saucepan until the butter is melted. Add the leeks and ginger and sauté until soft, stirring occasionally. Add the prawns to the pan and sauté until the flesh of the prawns turns pink and opaque, stirring occasionally.

Add the stock, lemon grass and seasoning and stir to mix. Bring to the boil and simmer for a couple of minutes. Remove and discard the lemon grass (or cool and freeze it to use at a later date).

Opposite: This Chilled Beetroot Borscht is garnished with grated cucumber, dill and sour cream

stuffed fruit and vegetables

What better way to jazz up fruit and vegetables than to stuff them? In the summer, a light lunch of some raw stuffed fruit is a favourite.

Avocados halved and stuffed with prawn cocktail are some children's (and adults') idea of heaven. But there are other combinations you can try – choosing the right stuffing is the secret of success, and different combinations will bring out the best flavours.

SPICY HERB-STUFFED SQUASH

This stuffing looks particularly attractive in a butternut squash – those orange bottle-shaped members of the marrow family – but you can use the stuffing for all types of squash.

SERVES 4

2 squash (about 1.5kg/3lb 5oz total weight)
4 tablespoons olive oil
1 onion, finely chopped
2 leeks, washed and finely chopped
4 cloves garlic, crushed
1 tablespoon wholegrain mustard
2 teaspoons chilli powder
2 teaspoons finely chopped fresh thyme
2 teaspoons finely chopped fresh sage
salt and freshly ground black pepper
115g (4oz) parmesan cheese, grated

Preheat the oven to 200°C/400°F/Gas Mark 6. Halve both the squash, then scoop out and discard the seeds. Cut out and reserve the flesh, taking care to leave a thick enough shell to contain the stuffing. Brush the squash shells with 2 tablespoons oil and place them in a roasting tin. Cover with greaseproof paper and bake in the oven for 15 minutes or until they are starting to soften.

Meanwhile, chop the reserved squash flesh and set aside. Heat the remaining oil in a frying pan, add the onion, leeks and garlic and cook for about 5 minutes, or until softened, stirring occasionally. Stir in the mustard and chilli powder.

Add the chopped squash, thyme, sage and seasoning to the onion mixture and stir to mix well. Cook for a further 5 minutes, stirring occasionally, then pile the mixture into the squash shells. Sprinkle with the parmesan cheese and bake in the oven for a further 10 minutes or until cooked. Serve.

APPLES STUFFED WITH PORK AND APRICOTS

The combination of flavours in this dish is wonderful, and organic apples and pork are even tastier! Use organic cider as well – it is now widely available.

SERVES 4

2 teaspoons olive oil
2 onions, finely chopped
5 firm large eating apples, such as Golden Delicious
350g (12oz) pork fillet, cut into 2.5cm (1in) cubes (or use lean minced pork)
4 ready-to-eat dried apricots, chopped
1 tablespoon chopped fresh parsley
salt and freshly ground black pepper
300ml (½ pint) dry or medium cider

Preheat the oven to 180°C/350°F/Gas Mark 4. Grease a shallow baking tin and set aside. Heat the oil in a heavy-based frying pan, add the onions and sauté until soft and browning, stirring occasionally.

Meanwhile, prepare the apples. Core 4 apples, leaving the peel on, then with a small sharp knife, cut the skin

Opposite: Pumpkin and squash are often underestimated, but in fact can be used to create many delicious dishes

around the top of each apple to make an opening of about 4–5cm (1½–2in), depending on the size of the apples. Hollow out the insides of the apples, taking care to leave thick sides.

Place the hollowed-out apples in the prepared baking tin, making sure they don't touch each other. Chop the apple flesh that you have just removed.

Place the softened onions, chopped apple flesh, pork, apricots, parsley and seasoning in a blender or food processor and blend until the meat is finely chopped. Stuff each prepared apple with some of the pork mixture, then bake in the oven for 15 minutes.

Peel, core and slice the remaining apple and arrange the apple slices around the stuffed apples in the tin. Pour the cider over the apples and bake for a further 15 minutes, or until the pork is cooked and browned and the fruit is soft. Serve.

MOROCCAN-STYLE STUFFED ONIONS

The aromatic flavours in this stuffing are enhanced by the sweet potato. I like to serve the onions on a bed of plain, well-seasoned rice, with their juices poured over it before placing the onions on top.

SERVES 4

4 large Spanish onions
1 tablespoon olive oil
2 cloves garlic, crushed
3 tablespoons sugar
½ teaspoon ground coriander
½ teaspoon ground cumin
½ teaspoon turmeric
salt and freshly ground black pepper
600ml (1 pint) vegetable stock
2 tablespoons raisins
225g (8oz) sweet potatoes, diced
100g (3½oz) pistachio nuts, shelled and roasted
chopped fresh parsley, to garnish

Preheat the oven to 200°C/400°F/Gas Mark 6. Peel the onions and carefully remove the centre of each one with a sharp knife. Set the onion cases to one side and chop the onion flesh that you have removed.

Heat the oil in a frying pan, add the chopped onion and sauté gently until soft, stirring occasionally. Add the garlic, sugar, coriander, cumin and turmeric and sauté for a further 1 minute, stirring. Season to taste with salt and pepper, then spoon the mixture into the onion cases.

Place the stuffed onions in a roasting tin, pour the stock over them, then sprinkle with the raisins. Bake in the oven for about 30 minutes or until the onions begin to soften and turn golden. Add the sweet potatoes to the tin, turning to coat them in the juices. Cook for a further 30 minutes or until the potatoes are cooked and the onions are caramelized. Garnish with the pistachio nuts and chopped parsley and serve with rice or crusty bread.

CRAB-STUFFED PAPAYA

The slightly sour taste of the filling offsets the sweetness of the papaya in this recipe.

SERVES 4

2 papaya
1 small cucumber or ½ standard cucumber, coarsely grated
225g (8oz) fresh or frozen (defrosted) crab meat
juice of 1 lemon
1 tablespoon finely chopped fresh coriander
salt and freshly ground black pepper

Cut the papaya in half and scrape out and discard the seeds. Place the fruit halves on a serving plate.

Place the cucumber, crab meat, lemon juice, chopped coriander and seasoning in a bowl and stir to mix well. Spoon the crab mixture into the papaya and serve.

Opposite: Moroccan-style Stuffed Onions served with sweet potatoes

MUSHROOMS STUFFED WITH THYME AND MOZZARELLA

I've become a mozzarella snob. The buffalo mozzarella we use in the restaurant is flown into London twice a week and it is one of life's great treats. Try it and see.

Mushrooms shrink quite considerably when cooked, so choose the biggest flat variety you can find. If you can't get them, use medium cup mushrooms but allow more per person.

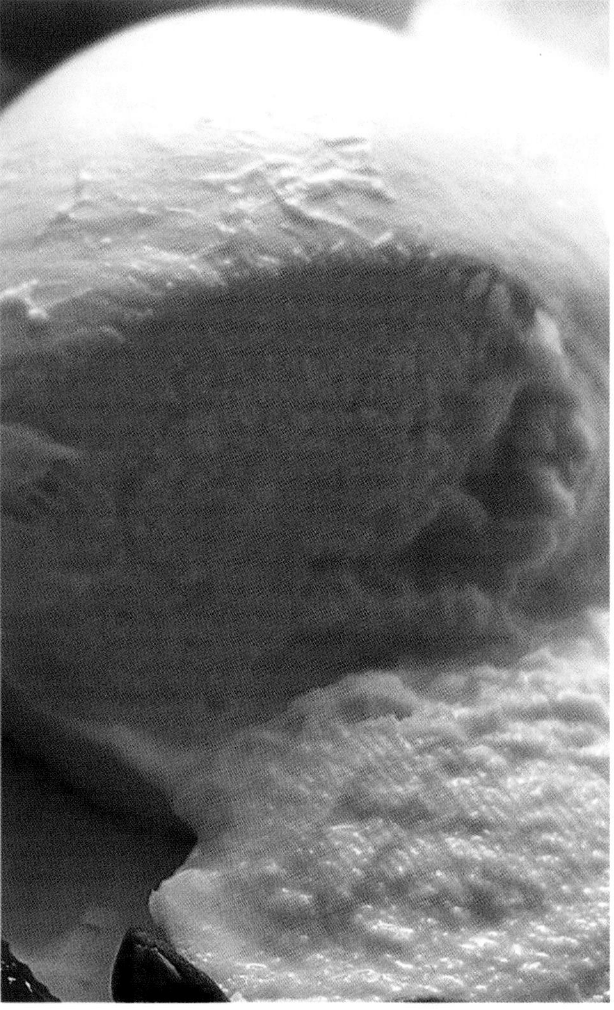

Below: Fresh Italian buffalo mozzarella is vastly superior to the usual vacuum packed alternative

SERVES 4 AS A LIGHT LUNCH

- 8 flat field mushrooms or 16 or more (depending on size) cup mushrooms, stalks removed
- 4 tablespoons olive oil
- juice of 1 lemon
- 1 teaspoon chopped fresh thyme
- salt and freshly ground black pepper
- 225g (8oz) fresh spinach or chard leaves
- 115g (4oz) buffalo mozzarella, sliced
- 1 tablespoon ground hazelnuts

Preheat the oven to 200°C/400°F/Gas Mark 6. Grease a large shallow ovenproof dish and set aside. Wipe the mushrooms, but do not wash them, then place them in the prepared dish. Mix the oil, lemon juice, thyme and salt and pepper together in a bowl, then pour this over the mushrooms.

Bake in the oven for 15 minutes. Meanwhile, wilt the spinach or chard leaves. To do this, wash the leaves thoroughly, then drop them into a saucepan, cover and cook over a medium heat for 2–3 minutes, shaking the pan occasionally. The leaves will cook in their own water so do not add any extra, otherwise you will make them mushy. Drain well, set aside to cool, then squeeze out the excess moisture with your hands.

Remove the mushrooms from the oven. Coarsely chop the spinach or chard leaves, then season them with salt and pepper. Spoon the spinach or chard mixture into the mushrooms.

Divide the mozzarella equally between the mushrooms, placing it on top of the spinach, then sprinkle with the ground hazelnuts. Return to the oven and bake for about 8 minutes or until the cheese has melted before serving. This dish is wonderful as an accompaniment to grilled meat or fish, too.

TOMATOES STUFFED WITH SPINACH AND PINE NUT RICOTTA

Make sure that the tomatoes you use are firm, otherwise they will collapse when you drain them. If you can't get large tomatoes – with organic produce you may be limited in your choice – use 3 smaller ones per person.

SERVES 4 AS A MAIN COURSE

- 8 large beefsteak tomatoes
- salt and freshly ground black pepper
- 3 tablespoons olive oil
- 1 onion, finely chopped
- 280g (10oz) cooked fresh spinach, well drained, or frozen spinach, defrosted and well drained
- grinding of nutmeg
- 225g (8oz) ricotta cheese
- 1 egg, beaten
- 115g (4oz) toasted pine nuts
- 115g (4oz) parmesan cheese, grated
- 1 tablespoon chopped fresh basil

Preheat the oven to 200°C/400°F/Gas Mark 6. Slice the tops off the tomatoes and scoop out and discard the seeds. Sprinkle the hollow insides with salt and leave upside down on absorbent kitchen paper for about 30 minutes to drain.

Meanwhile, heat the oil in a heavy-based frying pan, add the onion and cook until soft and golden, stirring occasionally. Make sure the spinach is thoroughly squeezed, then chop it and add to the onions. Season with salt and pepper and a grinding of nutmeg. Cook for a further 10 minutes, stirring occasionally, then remove the pan from the heat and set aside.

Place the ricotta in a bowl, add the egg and beat together until well mixed. Add the pine nuts and half the parmesan cheese and stir to mix. Add the spinach mixture and mix well. Place the tomato shells, cut side up, in a roasting tin and spoon the ricotta filling into them.

Sprinkle with the remaining parmesan, then bake in the oven for 15 minutes or until the filling is just beginning to brown and the tomatoes are soft but not collapsing. Sprinkle the chopped basil over the tomatoes and serve.

PIEDMONTESE STUFFED PEPPERS

This is a very simple recipe from the Piedmonte area of Italy. It can be served hot or cold. I have added cooked rice so that it can be served as a more substantial main dish.

SERVES 4

- 4 red peppers
- 4 cloves garlic, sliced
- salt and freshly ground black pepper
- 2 tablespoons olive oil
- 350g (12oz) cooked brown or white rice
- 50g (1¾oz) can anchovies, drained and crushed
- 1 tablespoon chopped pitted black olives
- 1 tablespoon chopped fresh oregano
- 4 plum or standard tomatoes, halved
- 2 tablespoons chopped fresh basil

Preheat the oven to 220°C/425°F/Gas Mark 7. Lightly oil a baking sheet and set aside. Halve the peppers and remove and discard the seeds but leave the stalks intact. Place the peppers, cut side up, on the baking sheet.

Place garlic slices inside the pepper halves and season with salt and pepper. Drizzle with oil, then bake in the oven for 10 minutes.

Meanwhile, mix the rice, anchovies, olives, oregano and seasoning together in a bowl. Remove the peppers from the oven and reduce the oven temperature to 200°C/400°F/Gas Mark 6. Fill the pepper halves with the rice mixture, then place the tomato halves on top.

Bake in the oven for a further 15 minutes or until the peppers are tender. Serve hot or cold, sprinkled with chopped basil.

top pasta sauces

In the time it takes to open a jar of pre-made pasta sauce you can dress your pasta yourself. Keep a good selection of different types of pasta in your cupboard, such as pasta made with wholemeal flour, spelt or rice.

To cook pasta, bring a large saucepan of lightly salted water (about 4.4 litres/8 pints) to the boil. Add about 2 teaspoons olive oil to the water, to prevent the pasta from sticking together.

For 4 people, select about 450–700g (1lb–1lb 9oz) fresh pasta or 350–450g (12oz–1lb) dried pasta of your choice (depending on the appetites of the eaters!) and drop it gradually into the water so that the water does not stop boiling. Stir and cook according to the manufacturer's or recipe instructions.

Make sure you take the pan off the heat before the pasta is just cooked, as while the pasta is hot it will continue to cook. The cooked pasta should be *al dente* – tender but still firm. You will need to test it with your teeth or fingernail. As a general rule, fresh pasta will cook in approximately 3–5 minutes and dried pasta in about 10–12 minutes. Drain thoroughly and serve with a pasta sauce of your choice.

LAST-MINUTE SAUCE

SERVES 4

- 1 tablespoon olive oil
- 1 clove garlic, crushed
- 1 tablespoon finely grated fresh parmesan cheese
- 1 teaspoon finely chopped fresh parsley
- 1 teaspoon finely chopped fresh oregano
- salt and freshly ground black pepper, to taste

Add all the above ingredients to the hot cooked pasta, toss to mix well, then serve.

Left: The deliciously simple Last-minute Sauce

BASIL AND PINE NUT SAUCE

This traditional pesto uses a lot of basil but you really need this much to capture the unique taste that has made this pasta sauce so popular. It is wonderful as a side sauce for chicken or fish too, or stirred into vegetable dishes. It will for keep up to 10 days in the fridge with a layer of olive oil on top.

SERVES 4

1 large bunch of fresh basil leaves (about 40)
3 cloves garlic, crushed
2 tablespoons pine nuts
2 tablespoons grated pecorino or parmesan cheese
pinch of salt
175ml (6fl oz) olive oil
freshly ground black pepper, to taste

Place the basil, garlic, pine nuts, cheese and salt in a blender or food processor and blend until smooth. With the motor still running, gradually add the oil until the sauce is smooth and creamy.

Season to taste with black pepper and serve with absolutely any type of hot cooked pasta.

MINT AND WALNUT SAUCE

This is a refreshing and interesting variation on the basil and pine nut pesto. It has a thicker texture because of the breadcrumbs. As with the traditional pesto, it can be used as a sauce for meats, fish and vegetables. Store in the same way as the basil pesto.

SERVES 4

115g (4oz) walnuts
28g (1oz) bread crumbs
175ml (6fl oz) olive oil
2 cloves garlic, peeled
85g (3oz) parmesan cheese, grated
1 bunch of fresh mint
1 tablespoon roughly chopped fresh basil
1 tablespoon roughly chopped fresh parsley
salt and freshly ground black pepper
fresh mint leaves, to garnish

Pulse a slice of fresh bread without the crust in a food processor until you have fairly fine crumbs, moisten with a tablespoon of the oil, then add the walnuts, roughly chopped, the garlic, basil, parsley, mint and parmesan. Pulse everything until it is finely chopped, but not too smooth or paste-like. The slightly rough-chopped texture will give a more interesting consistency. Gradually add in the oil until everything is mixed together.

Toss with freshly cooked pasta and garnish with the whole mint leaves.

TOP NUTS

You can experiment with other nuts for this sauce, or indeed just scatter chopped nuts on pasta with a drizzle of olive oil and some seasoning. The three top nuts, nutritionally speaking, are walnuts, Brazil nuts and almonds. For preference eat walnuts as these are rich in 'omega 3' (also found in some fish) a fatty acid believed to have beneficial effects on the heart and on circulation.

Nuts are part of a healthy diet, especially for vegetarians, as they are an excellent source of protein, minerals and 'good' fats.

Below: The fresh ingredients for two top pasta sauces, Basil and Pine Nut (below) and Walnut (bottom)

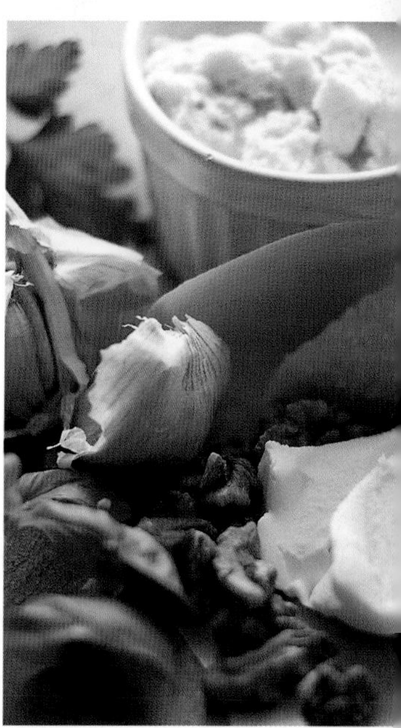

The ingredients for Vegetable and Prawn Sauce (above) and Chilli and Lentil Sauce (below)

VEGETABLE AND PRAWN SAUCE

This recipe comes from Bologna, which is the home of the pasta known as tortellini – those little stuffed parcels. This sauce is traditionally served with the mushroom-stuffed tortellini, but of course will go well with any pasta, especially spaghetti. Organic fresh chilled tortellini is now widely available. You will need at least 500g (1lb 2oz) fresh tortellini for 4 people. If using a different pasta, follow the manufacturer's guide for quantities.

SERVES 4

100g (3½oz) fresh (shelled) or frozen peas
55g (2oz) butter
2 courgettes, thinly sliced
100g (3½oz) rocket or baby spinach leaves, finely chopped
4 tablespoons dry white wine
250g (9oz) shelled fresh raw prawns or shrimps
125ml (4fl oz) single cream
500g (1lb 2oz) fresh tortellini
salt and freshly ground black pepper
½ teaspoon olive oil
20g (¾oz) finely chopped fresh dill (optional)

Cook the fresh peas in a saucepan of boiling water for 10 minutes. Drain well.

Melt the butter in a frying pan and add the cooked or defrosted peas, courgettes and rocket or spinach. Sauté for 5 minutes, stirring occasionally, then add the wine and prawns or shrimps and stir to mix. Cover and cook over a medium heat for about 5 minutes, or until the prawns or shrimps are cooked, shaking the pan occasionally. Stir in the cream, then remove the pan from the heat and set aside while you cook the pasta.

Cook the tortellini according to the packet instructions, in a large saucepan of lightly salted, boiling water to which the oil has been added. Drain the pasta, then place it in a warm serving bowl, add the prawn or shrimp sauce, chopped dill, if using, and salt and pepper, and toss to mix. Serve.

CHILLI AND LENTIL SAUCE

In the Campagna region, behind the Amalfi coast in the south-west of Italy, they eat this sauce with the little tube-shaped pasta called bucatini. Beware: this is not a light meal! For 4 people, use about 450g (1lb) bucatini or any other small pasta shapes.

SERVES 4

2 tablespoons olive oil
1 red onion, finely chopped
2 cloves garlic, chopped
1 fresh red chilli, deseeded and finely chopped (increase the quantity, if you like it hot)
4 small potatoes, cut into small pieces
2 carrots, finely chopped
two 400g (14oz) cans chopped tomatoes
225g (8oz) green lentils
375ml (13fl oz) dry white wine
450g (1lb) bucatini pasta
salt and freshly ground black pepper

Heat the oil in a large, heavy-based saucepan. Add the onion and sauté until soft, stirring occasionally. Add the garlic and chilli and cook until the onions are turning golden, stirring occasionally. Add the potatoes, carrots, tomatoes, lentils and wine and stir to mix. Bring to the boil, then cover and simmer for about 1½ hours, or until the lentils and vegetables are cooked and tender, stirring occasionally. Add a little water to the sauce at intervals during the cooking, so that it does not become too dry.

Meanwhile, cook the pasta in a large saucepan of lightly salted, boiling water until just cooked or *al dente*. Drain thoroughly and spoon onto serving plates or bowls. Season the lentil sauce with salt and pepper and spoon it over the pasta. Serve.

ROASTED CHILLI AND AUBERGINE SAUCE

Like the Chilli and Lentil Sauce (see recipe on previous page), this is a substantial dish traditionally served to hungry farmers returning from a hard day in the fields. Make sure your eaters have that sort of appetite!

SERVES 4

- 2 medium aubergines (approx 700g/1lb 9oz in total weight)
- 4 mild fresh chillies, deseeded and roughly chopped
- 8 cloves garlic, peeled
- 12 dried allspice berries, ground, or 1 teaspoon ground allspice
- salt and freshly ground black pepper
- 6 tablespoons olive oil
- 400g (14oz) crème fraîche
- 1 tablespoon chopped fresh flat-leaf parsley

Preheat the oven to 220°C/425°F/Gas Mark 7. Cut the aubergines into chunks about 2cm (¾in) in size. Place the aubergine chunks in a roasting tin with the chillies, garlic, allspice and salt and pepper. Drizzle with the oil, then roast in the oven for about 25 minutes, or until the aubergines are soft and toasted.

Meanwhile, cook your chosen pasta according to the packet instructions. Drain the pasta and return it to the saucepan. Add the crème fraîche to the roasted aubergines and add this mixture to the pasta in the pan. Stir to mix.

Add the parsley, adjust the seasoning to taste, and cook over a gentle heat for a few minutes or until the crème fraîche is warm, stirring. Serve.

PUTTANESCA

This roughly chopped, strong-flavoured, easy-to-prepare sauce is a universal favourite, partly, I'm sure, because of it's name which comes from *puttane* – Italian ladies of the night – making it just that little bit saucier! Use 450g (1lb) thin pasta, such as spaghetti or linguine.

SERVES 4

- 900g (2lb) tomatoes, skinned and chopped, or 2 x 400g (14oz) cans whole plum tomatoes, drained
- 2 tablespoons olive oil
- 55g (2oz) pitted black olives, chopped
- 25g (1oz) capers
- 8 canned anchovy fillets, drained and coarsely chopped
- 4 cloves garlic, finely chopped
- 2 teaspoons salt
- 1 teaspoon dried chilli flakes, or 1 small fresh chilli, deseeded and finely chopped
- 1 teaspoon chopped fresh oregano
- 2 tablespoons chopped fresh parsley

The ingredients for Roasted Chilli and Aubergine Sauce (above) and spicy Puttanesca (below)

Above: The ingredients for Oriental sauce. Opposite: The slow marinating of the ingredients yields a fresh, creamy Uncooked Goat's Cheese and Tomato Sauce

Place the tomatoes in a heavy-based saucepan with the oil and stir to mix. Bring the mixture to the boil, then add the olives, capers, anchovies, garlic, salt, chilli flakes or fresh chilli, oregano and half the parsley and stir to mix.

Reduce the heat slightly and continue to cook, stirring occasionally, while you cook your chosen pasta in a large saucepan of lightly salted, boiling water until just cooked or *al dente*.

Drain the pasta thoroughly, then place it on warmed serving plates. Spoon the sauce on top of the pasta and sprinkle with the remaining parsley. Serve.

ORIENTAL SAUCE

This sauce goes really well with linguine, tagliatelle or fettucine.

SERVES 4

- 2 onions or 8 spring onions, chopped
- 2 cloves garlic, chopped
- 1 tablespoon peeled grated fresh root ginger
- 2 fresh red chillies, deseeded and finely chopped, or 2 teaspoons chilli powder
- 1 tablespoon sesame oil
- 1 tablespoon olive oil
- 450g (1lb) tofu or skinless boneless chicken breasts, cut into 4cm (1½in) cubes
- salt and freshly ground black pepper
- 2 tablespoons soya sauce
- 2 tablespoons white wine vinegar
- 85g (3oz) beansprouts
- 4 tablespoons chopped fresh coriander

Place the onions or spring onions, garlic, ginger, chillies or chilli powder and sesame oil in a blender or food processor and blend to form a purée. Heat the olive oil in a wok, add the onion purée and stir-fry the purée until it starts to darken in colour slightly.

Add the tofu or chicken pieces and salt and pepper and stir-fry gently for 2 minutes. Add the soya sauce and vinegar and stir-fry for a further 10 minutes, or until the tofu or chicken is cooked and tender.

Add the beansprouts and stir-fry until hot, then add the chopped coriander and stir to mix. Serve with cooked linguine or noodles.

UNCOOKED GOAT'S CHEESE AND TOMATO SAUCE

The secret of this sauce is to let the ingredients marinate together for a least 2 hours before serving.

SERVES 4

- 225g (8oz) soft goat's cheese (such as goat's brie), crumbled into small pieces
- 4 large ripe tomatoes, cut into 5mm (¼in) cubes
- 3 cloves garlic, crushed
- 4 tablespoons olive oil
- 2 tablespoons chopped fresh basil
- 2 teaspoons salt
- ½ teaspoon freshly ground black pepper

Place all the ingredients in a large serving bowl and stir to mix. Cover with a clean cloth, set aside and leave to marinate at room temperature for at least 2 hours.

Cook the pasta of your choice and drain thoroughly. Add the goat's cheese sauce to the hot pasta, mix and serve immediately.

salads

We're not always very imaginative with salads in Britain. Mention salad to most people over the age of 50 and they will tell you that their childhood memory of it consists of lettuce leaves, tomatoes, spring onions and Heinz salad cream.

Yet raw vegetables are possibly the most important part of a healthy diet and a tasty salad is surely the best route to achieve this. But be sure to eat organic vegetables: only then can you be certain that they have not been sprayed with a cocktail of harmful pesticides. You can taste the difference too, particularly with carrots and apples.

To get the best from your fresh salad ingredients, simply rinse your green leaves in very cold water to crisp them, drain and whirl in a clean tea towel to dry. Dress with your favourite dressing (see recipes on page 15) or add a tablespoon of natural yoghurt to vary, or whizz the same dressing in a blender with some sesame seeds.

The recipes for summer salads need not necessarily be used as side salads – they can be a meal in themselves. Serve them together and you have the perfect light summer lunch menu.

Although we associate salads with summer, a warm winter salad can be a very welcome addition to the menu. There are numerous winter vegetables and storecupboard staples that can be transformed into invigorating salads. Whatever the season the following recipes will provide fresh, healthy options for family meals.

WALDORF SALAD

It may be very 1950s, but we love the crunchy, crisp texture of this salad and it is a great nutrition deliverer. It will serve 4 people for a light lunch, starter or buffet supper salad.

Opposite: This Waldorf Salad mixes fruit and nuts for a crisp starter

SERVES 4

4 firm, crisp eating apples
3 sticks celery, finely chopped
2 tablespoons Mayonnaise (see recipe on page 81)
2 tablespoons double cream, lightly whipped
squeeze of lemon juice
55g (2oz) walnuts, coarsely chopped

Wipe the apples, but do not peel them, then cut into quarters, core and dice them. Place the apples in a bowl with the celery and stir to mix.

Mix the mayonnaise and cream together and sharpen with a squeeze of lemon juice. Add to the apples at once and toss to mix to prevent the apples discolouring. Just before serving, stir in the walnuts.

TABBOULEH

This salad bursts with flavour yet is so simple to prepare.

SERVES 4

225g (8oz) bulghur wheat (cracked wheat)
2 spring onions, finely chopped
1 tomato, finely chopped
2 cloves garlic, crushed
2 tablespoons olive oil
2 teaspoons lemon juice
4 tablespoons finely chopped fresh parsley
2 tablespoons finely chopped fresh mint
½ teaspoon salt
freshly ground black pepper, to taste

Place the bulghur wheat in a bowl, add 350ml (12fl oz) warm water and stir to mix. Leave for about 30 minutes or until the water has been absorbed and the wheat is puffed out. Drain the bulghur wheat thoroughly, then squeeze it dry with your hands.

Place the bulghur wheat in a salad bowl, add all the remaining ingredients and toss to mix well. Serve immediately or cover and chill before serving.

PAPRIKA POTATOES ON A SALAD OF GREENS

This salad is a complete meal, giving a whole assortment of tastes. It is best made with new potatoes, but if these are not available, use medium-sized potatoes cut into bite-sized pieces.

SERVES 4

FOR THE SALAD:

16 new potatoes, cut into quarters, or 8 medium potatoes, cut into bite-sized pieces
1 tablespoon butter, melted
1 tablespoon olive oil
½ teaspoon salt
½ teaspoon paprika
225g (8oz) broccoli florets
1 cos or firm lettuce, torn into bite-sized pieces
115g (4oz) young or baby fresh spinach leaves
55g (2oz) white or red cabbage, thinly shredded
55g (2oz) alfalfa sprouts

FOR THE DRESSING:

2 tablespoons Mayonnaise (see recipe on page 81)
2 tablespoons lemon juice
2 teaspoons olive oil
2 teaspoons vegetable bouillon powder
1 clove garlic, crushed
freshly ground black pepper, to taste

Preheat the oven to 200°C/400°F/Gas Mark 6. Make the salad. Parboil the potatoes in a saucepan of boiling water for 5 minutes. Drain thoroughly then place in a bowl, add the butter, oil, salt and paprika and stir until the potatoes are coated all over.

Place the potatoes on a baking sheet and bake in the oven for 10–15 minutes, or until they are tender, but not mushy. Meanwhile, boil or steam the broccoli in or over a saucepan of boiling water for about 5 minutes or until it is just tender. Drain the broccoli well and set it aside.

Make the dressing. Place all the ingredients in a small bowl and stir until smooth and well mixed. Set aside.

Place the lettuce in a salad bowl with the spinach, cabbage and alfalfa sprouts. Slice the cooked broccoli thinly, add to the greens and toss to mix. Remove the potatoes from the oven and add to the salad. Pour over the dressing and toss to mix. Serve.

SEAFOOD SALAD

You can use a combination of seafoods for this salad. I have used a mixture of squid, prawns and mussels. For a more festive salad, garnish with some cooked king or tiger prawns.

SERVES 4

salt and freshly ground black pepper
225g (8oz) prepared squid, cleaned and sliced
450g (1lb) shelled fresh raw prawns
450g (1lb) mussels in their shells, scrubbed
115g (4oz) spring onions or shallots, finely chopped, plus extra to garnish
115g (4oz) tomato, finely chopped
55g (2oz) celery, finely chopped
2 tablespoons olive oil
2 teaspoons white wine vinegar
1 teaspoon dried oregano
115g (4oz) fresh (shelled) or frozen peas, cooked and drained
cooked king or tiger prawns, to garnish

Bring a large saucepan of salted water to the boil and drop in the squid, closely followed by the prawns and the mussels. Just before the water returns to the boil, pour the contents of the saucepan through a strainer set in the

Opposite: Seafood Salad garnished with tiger prawn

sink. Discard any mussels that have not opened and set the seafood aside to cool.

Make the dressing. Place the spring onions or shallots, tomato, celery, oil, vinegar, oregano and seasoning in a serving bowl and mix together thoroughly. Add the cooled seafood and peas and toss to mix. Serve garnished with king or tiger prawns and chopped spring onions or shallots.

POTATO SALAD TOSSED WITH MUSTARD AND TARRAGON SAUCE

Pep up your potato salad dressing with a dash of Dijon or wholegrain mustard, and if you can't find tarragon (which is the ideal herb for this dish) – and organic tarragon is scarce at any time of year – use any other fresh herb.

SERVES 4

FOR THE SALAD:

8 medium waxy potatoes or 16 new potatoes
1 red pepper, deseeded and diced
2 spring onions, finely chopped
2 hardboiled eggs, shelled and roughly chopped
55g (2oz) mixed toasted sunflower and sesame seeds
1 tablespoon finely chopped fresh parsley

FOR THE DRESSING:

225ml (8fl oz) Mayonnaise (see recipe on page 81)
2 tablespoons cider vinegar
2 teaspoons Dijon or wholegrain mustard
dash of soya sauce
2 teaspoons chopped fresh tarragon
1 teaspoon salt
freshly ground black pepper, to taste

Cook the potatoes in their skins in a saucepan of boiling water for about 15–20 minutes, or until they are tender but still firm and not mushy (you can save the water from the saucepan and use it later as a base for soup stock).

Drain and set aside to cool, then cut the potatoes into dice. If you are not particularly keen on potato skins, peel them first and then boil with a little fresh mint.

Place the diced potatoes in a salad bowl with all the remaining salad ingredients and toss to mix. Place all the dressing ingredients in a small bowl and stir together until well mixed.

Pour the dressing over the potato salad, toss to mix together and serve.

SPINACH AND BACON SALAD TOSSED IN SOUR CREAM AND BALSAMIC DRESSING

Fresh young organic spinach leaves tossed with crispy bacon are combined to create this delicious salad. The balsamic dressing is the perfect finishing touch.

SERVES 4

700g (1lb 9oz) young or baby spinach leaves
4 rashers lean back bacon, diced
1 clove garlic, finely chopped
2 tablespoons olive oil
1 tablespoon sour cream
1 tablespoon balsamic vinegar
salt and freshly ground black pepper
2 spring onions, finely chopped

Roll up the spinach leaves and slice them very thinly with a sharp knife, cutting them into shreds. Set aside.

Place the diced bacon in a dry frying pan and toss over a medium heat until it is nicely frizzled. Add the spinach and toss for about 1 minute. Turn the bacon pieces and spinach into a salad bowl.

Place the garlic, oil, sour cream, vinegar and seasoning in a small bowl and whisk together until thoroughly mixed. Pour the dressing over the spinach and bacon and toss to mix.

Sprinkle the spring onions over the salad to garnish and serve immediately.

MIXED BEANS WITH A CAPER AND HERB SAUCE

For this recipe, take about 350g (12oz) of any dried beans you like: these can be black-eyed beans, pinto beans, lima beans or whatever takes your fancy. You can also buy mixed bean packs with up to 10 different varieties. Whatever you choose, try to get an interesting mix of colours.

The key to cooking dried beans is to soak them for about 12 hours – overnight is a good rule of thumb.

SERVES 4

350g (12oz) mixed dried beans
salt and freshly ground black pepper
½ red or white onion, chopped
4 cloves garlic, chopped
90ml (3fl oz) olive oil
2 tablespoons capers
3 tablespoons red wine vinegar
1 teaspoon sugar
3 tablespoons chopped fresh flat-leaf parsley
1 tablespoon chopped fresh oregano
mixed salad leaves, to serve

Place the mixed beans in a large bowl and cover with plenty of cold water. Leave to soak overnight, then rinse and drain.

Place the beans in a large saucepan, cover with fresh water and add 1 teaspoon of salt. Bring to the boil, then cover and simmer gently for about 45 minutes or until tender.

Meanwhile, place all the remaining ingredients, except the salad leaves, in a blender or food processor and blend or pulse in short bursts to chop the ingredients roughly – the result should not be a smooth sauce.

Tip the caper mixture into a large bowl. Drain the cooked beans thoroughly, then add them to the bowl and toss to mix thoroughly. Serve on a mixed leaf salad, which should include rocket if you can find it!

MAYONNAISE

There are several ways to create a classic mayonnaise, but this is my version.

MAKES 300ml (½ pint)

2 eggs
1 teaspoon mixed sea salt (or vegetable stock powder) and freshly ground black pepper
1 teaspoon Dijon mustard
100ml (3½fl oz) olive oil
100ml (3½fl oz) sunflower oil
2 tablespoons cider vinegar

Place the eggs together with the sea salt and pepper (or stock powder) and mustard in a blender or food processor. Start the motor running and combine these ingredients with a short whizz. With the motor running, start adding oil in thin stream, using the olive oil first, followed by the sunflower oil. When it begins to thicken, add the vinegar. Turn off the motor as soon as the vinegar is incorporated. Use immediately or store in a covered container in the refrigerator for up to 3 days.

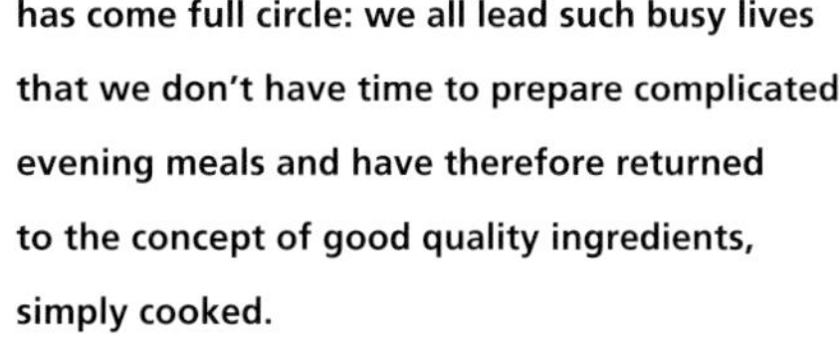

simple suppers

When I was a growing up, we ate simple food. The evening meal was either high tea – something hot on toast and a piece of cake or pie to follow – or a simple supper dish, such as the lentil soup which my father always cooked on Sunday evening. As ingredients became more readily available after World War II people revelled in the riches and cooked elaborate creamy sauces, pies and pastries. Now the world has come full circle: we all lead such busy lives that we don't have time to prepare complicated evening meals and have therefore returned to the concept of good quality ingredients, simply cooked.

This can be a good thing. Simple food is healthier food – as long as the ingredients are whole, natural and organic. When you use these healthy ingredients, feeding your family properly becomes so much easier. So, in the following chapter I have devised a variety of simple supper (or high tea) dishes which are all tasty, full of goodness and easy to prepare.

Your family also needs to eat plenty of fresh fruit and vegetables every day, so make sure they finish their meals with an apple, pear or some other fruit. Or make a simple salad to accompany these supper dishes, and sprinkle over them vitamin-rich fresh green herbs such as parsley, chives and coriander.

Even though something like organic baked beans on wholegrain toast (see recipe on page 84) could hardly be simpler to make, if you really haven't got time to prepare something, try to buy organic ready-made dishes that have no harmful additives and don't contain high levels of sugar and salt. Again, chop a few home-grown herbs over the food for a more home-spun touch and add a few frozen organic vegetables to the meal. And you can't go wrong by finishing the family supper with a piece of fruit for dessert.

on toast

My abiding memory of coming home from school was the smell of toast and Marmite. Some time later I remember giving my own children mashed sardines on toast for tea in a hurry.

If the bread you are toasting is made from 100 per cent wholemeal stoneground organic flour, then this is a healthy base on which to construct a fast meal. If the bread you are using is made from pesticide-sprayed wheat which has then been refined and bleached, it isn't.

Hot toast spread with melting butter is hard to beat, but for a healthier option rub the toast with a little peeled garlic and the cut side of half a tomato, then drizzle with a little olive oil – but not, of course, as the basis for a banana buttie!

HOME-MADE BAKED BEANS

For quick baked beans on toast, use organic canned beans – some are sweetened with apple juice so they don't have the high sugar content of normal baked beans. But make your own beans, even if only once, for the fun of it! The use of molasses here instead of sugar gives them a high vitamin B content.

SERVES 4

450g (1lb) small dried haricot beans
1 tablespoon olive oil
1 large onion, chopped
4 tablespoons black treacle or molasses
2 tablespoons tomato purée
salt
½ teaspoon mustard powder
4 slices of bread, toasted

Place the beans in a bowl and add enough cold water to cover the beans well. Leave to soak overnight, then drain well.

Place the soaked beans in a saucepan and add enough cold water to cover. Bring to the boil and simmer for 5 minutes, then drain. Rinse the beans well under cold running water and return them to the pan, cover with cold water and boil once more for 1-1½ hours, until they are cooked but firm. Reserve the water.

Preheat the oven to 170°C/325°F/Gas Mark 3. Heat the olive oil in a pan and sauté the onion until soft, add the treacle or molasses, tomato purée, salt, mustard powder and enough of the drained water from the beans to make up 1.2 litres (2 pints) of liquid. Place the

Left: Bring back baked beans! Just make sure they're organic and served on healthy, wholemeal toast.

beans in an overproof dish and pour the liquid over them. Check the seasoning then cover and bake in the oven for 1 hour, until the sauce has thickened and the beans have turned a reddish brown. Spoon the baked beans over hot toast.

PEANUT BUTTER AND BANANA

This is a great favourite with the kids and men I know. Spread slices of toast with crunchy organic peanut butter and top with thick slices of totally different-tasting peeled organic bananas. Enjoy!

CHICKEN MAYONNAISE

I like to serve this on a bed of salad leaves, which have been drizzled with a little dressing. Just shred some cooked chicken and mix with mayonnaise – shop-bought or home-made (see page 81). Top the toast with dressed salad leaves if liked, spoon some chicken mayonnaise on top, garnish with chopped fresh parsley and serve.

GARLIC MUSHROOMS AND PARMESAN

The number of mushrooms needed for this dish will vary according to their size. Organic mushrooms are very nutritious, providing some protein and a range of vitamins and minerals, making them an excellent food for vegetarians and vegans.

SERVES 4

55g (2oz) butter
8 mushrooms (about 225g/8oz total weight), roughly chopped
1 tablespoon Worcestershire sauce
1 tablespoon chopped fresh parsley
salt and freshly ground black pepper
4 slices of bread
1 tablespoon grated or shaved fresh parmesan cheese

Preheat the grill to high. Melt the butter in a frying pan, add the mushrooms and sauté until softened, stirring occasionally. Stir in the Worcestershire sauce, parsley and seasoning.

Meanwhile, toast the bread on both sides. Spoon the mushroom mixture over the toast and sprinkle the parmesan over the top. Brown under the grill if liked, before serving.

WELSH RAREBIT

Or Caws Pobi – 'cooked cheese' – as it is called in God's Own Country (Wales!).

SERVES 4

175g (6oz) cheddar cheese (mild or strong, according to your taste), grated
6 tablespoons milk or beer
25g (1oz) butter
1 teaspoon English mustard
½ teaspoon Worcestershire sauce
a pinch of cayenne pepper
salt and freshly ground black pepper
4 slices of bread
fresh chives, to garnish

Preheat the grill to high. Place the cheese and milk or beer in a saucepan and heat gently until melted, stirring. Add the butter, mustard, Worcestershire sauce, cayenne pepper, salt and pepper, and continue to heat gently until the mixture is melted and well blended, stirring.

Toast the bread on one side and pour the cheese mixture onto the untoasted sides. Brown under the hot grill, then garnish with chives.

Above: Peanut Butter and Banana (top), Garlic Mushroom and Parmesan (centre) and Welsh Rarebit (bottom)

real fish

Fish makes a fast and healthy choice for supper and is very popular with children – think of fish fingers. Yet, surprisingly for an island nation, we eat very little fish compared to the rest of Europe. Fish is cheap and healthy, and not always bony!

FISH PIE

Children love this traditional fish pie made with firm white fish and hardboiled eggs. I like to use a mixture of smoked and unsmoked fish, and for a more festive pie I add in a bit of organically farmed salmon (see page 16).

SERVES 4

450g (1lb) cod fillet
225g (8oz) smoked haddock fillet
150ml (¼ pint) milk
a slice of lemon
2 bay leaves
55g (2oz) butter
25g (1oz) plain flour
2 eggs, hardboiled, shelled and chopped
2 tablespoons chopped fresh parsley
salt and freshly ground black pepper
700g (1lb 9oz) potatoes, boiled, drained, then mashed with a little butter and cream

Preheat the oven to 190°C/375°F/Gas Mark 5. Grease an ovenproof pie dish and set aside. Cut the fish into largish pieces and place in a saucepan with the milk, 150ml (¼ pint) water, the lemon and bay leaves. Bring to the boil, cover and simmer gently for about 10 minutes or until the fish is cooked. Strain off the cooking liquid and reserve 300ml (½ pint) for the sauce. Set aside. Remove and discard the skin and any bones from the fish and flake the flesh into large flakes. Set aside.

Make the sauce. Melt half the butter in a saucepan, add the flour and cook for 1 minute, stirring. Gradually add the reserved cooking stock, whisking well until smooth. Bring slowly to the boil, stirring, then simmer gently for 2–3 minutes.

Remove the pan from the heat and stir in the flaked fish, chopped eggs, parsley and seasoning. Spoon the mixture into the prepared dish and cover the top with the mashed potatoes. Fork the potato topping into ridges and dot with the remaining butter. Bake on the top shelf in the oven for 20–25 minutes or until the topping is golden brown. Serve.

MEDITERRANEAN FRIED SQUID

Variety in food is instilled at an early age – once you give in to the repeated assertions that children don't like this or that, you are setting up patterns of behaviour that will be hard to change. Try to shop with your children in fresh food markets and ethnic food quarters – this in itself is a whole education (my family grew up with a Spanish market as the centre of their eating), then take the food home and cook it with them.

If anything conjures up that perfect Mediterranean holiday, with the warm sea lapping at your toes and iced sangria clinking in the jug, it is these crisp round bites of fried squid. Buy whole squid as it comes from the sea with its squelchy innards and ink sac, and show your children how to clean it – dare you! – if not, buy it ready prepared.

SERVES 4

1.1kg (2½lb) squid or 900g (2lb) ready-prepared squid
225g (8oz) plain flour
1 teaspoon salt
225ml (8fl oz) sparkling water
450ml (16fl oz) sunflower oil, for frying
125ml (4fl oz) olive oil
2 lemons, cut into wedges, to serve

Opposite: Even those who generally turn up their noses at fish are unable to resist this traditional Fish Pie

Clean the squid, or if you can't face it have them cleaned for you (or buy ready prepared). To clean the squid, pull out the innards and discard the ink sac and hard bone from the back. Cut the small tentacles from the sac and keep these to use. Turn the squid inside out and rinse under warm running water until clean. Take a sharp knife and cut the squid across into circles about 1cm (½in) thick. Cut the tentacles into slices. If using ready-prepared squid, simply cut the squid into bite-sized circles.

Mix the flour and salt together on a large plate and pour the sparkling water into a bowl. Heat the oils together in a wok, deep-frying pan or deep-fat fryer until they are hot – test by dropping in a little water, when the oils should pop.

Working in small batches at a time, dip the squid first in the flour and salt, then quickly into the sparkling water and then place in the hot oil. Deep-fry over a medium heat for 5–8 minutes, or until crisp and golden. Drain on absorbent kitchen paper and keep hot while cooking the remaining squid. Serve hot with lemon wedges.

HOME-MADE FISH FINGERS

Many families regard fish fingers as a staple for children's teas – indeed, we spend over £100 million on them every year! Yet in many cases the fish content in these fingers makes up less than half of the product, and the coating is that yellow colour because it has been dyed. Better to make your own, and it's dead easy, so choose fresh firm white fish and go for it!

SERVES 4

- 700g (1lb 9oz) cod or haddock fillets
- 1 teaspoon salt
- 140g (5oz) fresh white or brown breadcrumbs
- ¼ teaspoon freshly ground black pepper
- 1 tablespoon chopped fresh mixed herbs (optional)
- 2 eggs, beaten
- 3 tablespoons olive oil

Cut the fish into fish-finger size shapes and sprinkle them all over with half the salt. On a sheet of greaseproof paper, mix the breadcrumbs with the remaining salt, the pepper and chopped herbs, if using.

Dip the fish fingers into the beaten egg and then into the breadcrumb mixture, pressing them in firmly and covering the fish all over. Repeat this dipping and coating process to make a substantial coating.

Heat the oil in a heavy-based frying pan, then add the fish fingers and fry for about 10 minutes, or until cooked and golden brown, turning once. Serve with Oven Chips (see recipe on page 90) – this will cut down on the fat used for frying – broccoli florets and Tomato Ketchup (see recipe on page 15).

Opposite: These home-made fish fingers are the healthy option. If you haven't got any time at all, simply grill small pieces of fish and serve with tomato ketchup

the humble spud

Potatoes – when organically grown – are an important part of our diet. They are a good source of vitamin C and potassium, as well as other minerals.

Tests on organic and non-organic potatoes have shown the organic version to contain approximately 25 per cent more zinc than non-organic. This depletion is due to repeated treatments with pesticides and fungicides (as with all non-organic crops) while the plants are growing, and then again after harvesting so that they can be stored for long periods.

As, after harvest, these pesticides and fungicides are sprayed directly on the potato skin, you can only safely eat this part of the vegetable when the potatoes are organic – and it is the skin which contains most of the nutrients!

Everybody loves chips. They are, quite simply, the world's favourite food – whether they're known as fries, *frites* or *patatas fritas*. There's just one problem: potato chips absorb lots of oil while they are being deep-fried, which makes them highly fattening.

However, I don't want to be a kill-joy: there's no reason why we can't all enjoy chips occasionally. But it makes sense, too, to cook the chips in different, healthier ways. After all, organic potatoes should be cooked to enhance their flavour, such as by sautéing them with onions and garlic in a little olive oil, or oven-roasting them with a light covering of oil, sea salt and freshly ground black pepper.

This way, we cut down on the amount of oil absorbed by the starchy potatoes, too – an extra bonus for health. And, I may add, oven-roasting chips is much, much easier than deep-frying them in a chip pan. If your family complains (they won't, but if they do), then I can only say '*nil carborundum*' – don't let them grind you down!

OVEN CHIPS

The simplest and most nutritious way of cooking chips is simply this. Preheat the oven to 230°C/450°F/Gas Mark 8. Cut scrubbed, unpeeled potatoes into 1cm (½in) thick chips. Pour a small amount of olive oil into a shallow baking tin and heat for a few minutes in the oven until hot.

Toss the chips in the oil until coated all over, then sprinkle with a little coarse salt. Bake in the oven for about 25 minutes, or until cooked and golden brown, turning occasionally.

You could add chopped fresh or dried herbs or even a sprinkling of chilli powder to the chips while cooking, to ring the changes.

SWEET POTATO CHIPS

Prepare as above, but peel the potatoes as the skins on sweet potatoes are much tougher. Cut the potatoes into chunky crescent shapes, drizzle with olive oil, then sprinkle with salt and a few sesame seeds before baking as above.

ROASTED CHEESE FANTAIL POTATOES

This method of roasting potatoes comes from the Hasselback restaurant in Sweden and they are gorgeous to look at. Eat on their own or as a potato accompaniment without the cheese.

SERVES 4

8 medium potatoes, peeled
55g (2oz) butter, melted
salt
1 teaspoon dried breadcrumbs
4 tablespoons grated cheese such as cheddar or gruyère

Preheat the oven to 220°C/425°F/Gas Mark 7. Lightly grease an ovenproof dish or baking tin and set aside. Cut the potatoes across their width, like a concertina, at 5mm

(¼in) intervals, three-quarters of the way through. To make this easier to do, the Hasselback restaurant pushes a skewer through the bottom of the horizontal potato, cuts down to that and then removes the skewer before cooking.

Place the potatoes in the prepared dish or tin and brush all over with melted butter. Sprinkle with salt and roast in the oven for 30 minutes.

Sprinkle with the breadcrumbs and cheese, then roast in the oven for a further 10 minutes or until golden and crisp. Serve.

GRATIN DAUPHINOIS

When I first tasted this dish in France it was 1958 and cream was still a luxury in Europe – most British families used evaporated milk as a substitute – so this dish was served on its own as a first course, before roast meat or chicken, which was followed by a simple green salad.

The best potatoes to use for this dish are waxy, firm varieties – or what the French call 'yellow' potatoes. If you cannot find these – and with organics it can be difficult always to get the variety you want – then use whatever potatoes you have.

SERVES 6

700g (1lb 9oz) potatoes
1 clove garlic, peeled
55g (2oz) butter
salt and freshly ground black pepper
1 egg
300ml (½ pint) double cream or milk

Preheat the oven to 190°C/375°F/Gas Mark 5. Peel the potatoes and cut them into very thin slices using a sharp knife or mandoline. Pat dry in a clean cloth or with absorbent kitchen paper. Roughly crush the garlic and rub it around an ovenproof dish, then grease the dish with half the butter.

Layer the potatoes in the dish, seasoning between each layer. Beat the egg with more seasoning and the cream or milk. Pour the egg mixture over the potato slices, lifting them gently so that the mixture runs between the layers to the bottom of the dish. Dot the remaining butter over the surface.

Bake on the top shelf of the oven for about 1 hour or until the potatoes are cooked and tender (test with a knife) and the top is crisp and brown. Serve with absolutely anything, or eat on its own!

POMMES BOULANGERE

We cook this dish often at home and in the restaurant, because it is so popular. If you have any fresh herbs, chop and mix some into the stock and sprinkle the rest on top before serving.

SERVES 6

55g (2oz) butter
700g (1lb 9oz) potatoes, thinly sliced
1 onion, thinly sliced
salt and freshly ground black pepper
300ml (½ pint) chicken or vegetable stock

Preheat the oven to 190°C/375°F/Gas Mark 5. Butter a shallow ovenproof pie dish such as a white fluted tart dish.

Arrange the potato and onion slices in alternate layers in the prepared dish, seasoning each layer with a little salt and pepper as you go and finishing with a layer of potatoes arranged in overlapping slices.

Dot the remaining butter over the surface. Pour in the stock, then bake in the oven for 1–1½hours or until the potatoes are tender and browned on top. Serve.

root vegetable cakes

These vegetable cakes can be adapted to use up any leftovers and are another way of serving potatoes and other root vegetables, either as an accompaniment or on their own with a tasty sauce. The trick with these patties is not to make them too dense or too thick.

POTATO AND CELERIAC CAKES WITH SALSA VERDE

The reason I have included a celeriac recipe is not because it is a vegetable you would often buy, but because it is one that is often found in seasonal organic veggie boxes and produces much head scratching over what to do with it.

SERVES 4

500g (1lb 2oz) potatoes, cut into chunks
55g (2oz) butter
4 cloves garlic, thinly sliced
225g (8oz) celeriac, coarsely grated
2 tablespoons wholegrain mustard
1 teaspoon finely chopped fresh thyme
2 eggs, beaten
plain flour, for dusting
2 tablespoons olive oil

Cook the potatoes in a saucepan of boiling water for about 15–20 minutes or until tender. Drain well, then mash the potatoes and set aside. (The mash should be dry, so do not add any milk or butter to it. To achieve a dry mash, it is quite a good idea to bake the potatoes in their jackets rather than boil them, then scrape the potato flesh out of the skins and mash it.)

Melt the butter in a frying pan, add the garlic and celeriac and cook for about 5 minutes, or until softened and golden, stirring occasionally. Remove the pan from the heat, add the mustard and thyme, then stir in the mashed potatoes and eggs, mixing well. Set aside until the mixture is cool enough to handle.

Flour your hands and form the mixture into 4 large patties about 2.5cm (1in) thick. Heat the oil in a frying pan, then add the potato cakes and fry until golden brown on both sides, turning once. Drain on absorbent kitchen paper and serve hot with Salsa Verde (see below).

SALSA VERDE

SERVES 4

1 large bunch of fresh flat-leaf parsley
1 large handful of fresh basil leaves
1 tablespoon roughly chopped fresh mint
2 cloves garlic, halved
1 tablespoon Dijon mustard
2 tablespoons capers, rinsed
6 tablespoons olive oil
1 tablespoon lemon juice
freshly ground black pepper

Place all the ingredients, except the oil, lemon juice and black pepper in a blender or food processor and blend until well mixed.

With the motor running, gradually add the oil in a steady stream until well mixed. Spoon into a bowl, stir in the lemon juice and season to taste with black pepper.

PARSNIP AND RED ONION CAKES WITH ANCHOÏADE

I am a great parsnip fan and this combination, served with anchovy sauce, makes a very unusual supper dish.

SERVES 4–6

450g (1lb) parsnips, roughly chopped
salt and freshly ground black pepper

Opposite: Potato and Celeriac Cakes with Salsa Verde

- 85g (3oz) butter
- 225g (8oz) red onions, chopped
- 2 cloves of garlic, crushed
- ½ teaspoon ground nutmeg
- 1–2 tablespoons plain flour, plus extra for dusting
- 2 tablespoons olive oil

Cook the parsnips in a large saucepan of lightly salted, boiling water for 10–15 minutes or until tender. Drain well, mash with 25g (1oz) butter and set aside.

Meanwhile, melt 25g (1oz) butter in a frying pan, add the onions and garlic and cook until softened, stirring occasionally. Add the onion mixture to the mashed parsnips and mix well. Add the nutmeg and season to taste with salt and pepper. Stir in enough flour to bind the mixture lightly together. Set aside until the mixture is cool enough to handle.

Flour your hands and form the mixture into 10–12 patties each about 5cm (2in) in diameter and 2.5cm (1in) thick. Heat the remaining butter and oil in a frying pan until the butter is melted, then add the patties and fry for 3–4 minutes on each side, or until golden brown, turning once. Drain on absorbent kitchen paper and serve hot with Anchoïade (see recipe below).

ANCHOÏADE

SERVES 4

- 115g (4oz) fresh anchovy fillets or two 50g (1¾oz) cans anchovies, drained and rinsed
- 2 cloves garlic, crushed
- 6 pitted black olives
- 1 tablespoon olive oil
- 1 tablespoon white wine vinegar

Place all the ingredients in a blender or food processor and blend until well mixed. Spoon into a dish and serve. Alternatively, this recipe is fun to make using the traditional method with a pestle and mortar. Try it this way to show your kids how things used to be done (and by purists, still are).

burgers

Meat and veggie burgers are the natural choice for your freezer. Freeze them raw, layered with greaseproof paper. You can take out as many as you need, one at a time, to feed what is becoming increasingly normal, the mixed-diet family – where some members are vegetarians, some carnivores. Freeze for up to 3 months.

PRETEND BURGER

About 10 years ago, my husband and I were full-time environmental campaigners. One day we hatched a great campaign with singer Chrissie Hynde of the Pretenders to challenge the mighty burger giants. Chrissie is a passionate vegetarian – and ranching beef to supply the steak and burger chains has destroyed tens of thousands of square miles of tropical forest in Central and South America. So, we decided to produce the world's most delicious, nutritious and irresistible veggie-burgers – to woo the customers away from the burger chains, and save both the cows and the forests.

For reasons I won't go into now, our plan never went into action. But here is a similar recipe for wonderful, protein-rich, lip-smacking, earth-friendly burgers made entirely from vegetable ingredients. Your kids will never want to go into a burger joint again – honest!

SERVES 4–6

- 175g (6oz) green lentils
- salt and freshly ground black pepper
- 1 small onion, grated
- 1 stick celery, grated
- 1 small carrot, grated
- 115g (4oz) ground mixed nuts

Opposite: The earth-friendly Pretend Burger served with onion rings and salad in a bun

2 cloves garlic, crushed
1 teaspoon finely chopped fresh or dried thyme
1 teaspoon finely chopped fresh or dried sage
1 teaspoon cayenne pepper
½ teaspoon mustard – any type
2 dashes of Worcestershire sauce
85g (3oz) fresh wholemeal breadcrumbs
1 egg, beaten
rolled oats, for coating
olive oil, for frying

Cook the lentils in a covered saucepan of lightly salted, boiling water for about 1 hour, or until cooked and tender. Drain well.

Preheat the oven to 220°C/425°F/Gas Mark 7. Place the cooked lentils and all the remaining ingredients, except the rolled oats and olive oil, in a bowl and stir until well mixed.

Form the mixture into 4–6 large, flat patties, then coat each burger all over with some rolled oats. Heat a little oil in a frying pan, add the burgers and cook gently for about 2–3 minutes on each side, or until golden brown, turning once.

Transfer the burgers to a baking sheet and bake in the oven for about 5 minutes, or until cooked and crisp on the outside. Serve.

CLASSIC BEEFBURGER

Beefburgers are so easy to make, no wonder they are the ultimate fast food. The quality of the burger depends simply on the quality of the meat – it needs to be organic, of course, and lean but not totally without fat otherwise it will fall apart, so enlist your butcher's help with this. If you are mincing your own meat, choose chuck steak, which is about 80 per cent lean meat and 20 per cent fat.

Burgers are also a good way to slip in lettuce, tomatoes and pickled cucumber for that daily dose of vegetables. Serve with organic tomato ketchup – there are several on the market now.

MAKES 4 BURGERS

450g (1lb) lean minced beef
2 teaspoons salt
¼ teaspoon freshly ground black pepper
25g (1oz) butter
1 tablespoon olive oil

Place the minced beef and seasoning in a bowl and stir together until well mixed, then shape into 4 round, flat patties each about 2.5cm (1in) thick. Heat the butter and oil in a frying pan and when sizzling, quickly fry the burgers for about 3–4 minutes on each side, or until cooked to your liking, turning once. Serve plain, with a topping, in a bun, or however you wish. These beefburgers go superbly with our home-made Tomato Ketchup (see recipe on page 15).

If you are serving the burgers with potatoes and not in a bun, you can make a quick gravy in the frying pan after you have removed the cooked burgers. Keep the burgers hot, then simply add a few tablespoons boiling stock (for quick stock, see page 14) or half stock, half wine, to the frying pan and stir in all the meaty bits left in the bottom of the pan. Bring to the boil, then season to taste with salt and pepper. Serve with the burgers.

You can, of course, grill the burgers if you would rather not fry them. Just brush them with a little oil, then grill them under a preheated hot grill for a few minutes on each side, or until cooked to your liking, turning once.

CHICKPEA BURGERS

Chickpeas are always in my storecupboard, either in tins or dried, and so this is a great recipe to have available when all other provisions are running low!

SERVES 4–6

450g (1lb) dried chickpeas or two 400g (14oz) cans chickpeas, rinsed and drained
2 medium potatoes, boiled, drained and mashed

1 onion, finely chopped
2 cloves garlic, crushed
2 tablespoons soya sauce
2 teaspoons lemon juice
freshly ground black pepper
plain wholemeal flour, for dusting
sunflower oil, for frying

If you are using dried chickpeas, place them in a bowl, cover with cold water and leave to soak overnight. Drain, then place the chickpeas in a large pan and cover with fresh cold water. Bring to the boil, then cover and simmer for about 1 hour, or until cooked and tender. Rinse, drain well, then set aside to cool.

Mash the cooked or canned chickpeas in a bowl with a fork or roughly chop them in a blender or food processor, then place them in a bowl. Add the mashed potatoes, onion, garlic, soya sauce, lemon juice and black pepper and mix well.

Flour your hands, then shape heaped tablespoonfuls of the mixture into small round, flat burgers. Dust each burger all over with a little flour.

Heat a little oil in a frying pan, add the burgers and fry gently for about 4 minutes on each side, or until cooked and golden, turning once. Serve with Spicy Burger Sauce (see recipe below), or in a bun with tomato ketchup and fresh tomatoes.

SPICY BURGER SAUCE

For young children you may need to omit the chilli in this spicy sauce.

SERVES 4

300ml (½ pint) vegetable stock
2 tablespoons tomato purée
1 tablespoon olive oil
1 tablespoon cider vinegar
1 tablespoon sugar
1 teaspoon chilli powder
1 clove garlic, crushed
salt and freshly ground black pepper

Place all the ingredients in a saucepan and stir to mix. Bring to the boil, then reduce the heat and simmer, uncovered, for 15 minutes, stirring occasionally. Serve.

no-dough pizzas

Pizza must be the most popular home-delivery dish ever, but not only is it bad value, it is also not particularly nutritious unless you make it yourself. However, waiting for dough to rise is not a simple supper option. Here are some tasty alternatives which you don't need to wait for.

When making these pizzas, choose and prepare the topping before making the base.

Above and opposite: These pizzas are easy and fun to make. Children can always be enticed to help if you let them have a go with the rolling pin!

POTATO PIZZETTA

I cannot tell you why the people of Apulia – at the foot of Italy, where durum wheat (pizza-grade flour cereal) is produced – are so fond of *pizzetta di patate*, but they are and here's their recipe for you to enjoy, too. This pizza base is particularly good with Bacon and Onion topping (see recipe on page 103).

SERVES 4 (MAKES 4 PIZZETTA)

500g (1lb 2oz) floury medium potatoes, left whole and unpeeled
salt
100g (3½oz) plain flour, plus extra for dusting
1 egg, beaten
1 tablespoon olive oil
grated nutmeg, to taste (optional)

Cook the potatoes in a saucepan of lightly salted, boiling water for about 20–30 minutes, or until tender. Drain and set aside until cool enough to handle, then peel the potatoes and place them in a bowl (I like to return the peelings to the potato water, which I then use for soup or sauce stock).

Preheat the oven to 220°C/425°F/Gas Mark 7. Mash the potatoes, add the flour, egg and oil, then season with a little salt and grated nutmeg, if using, and with your hands work the ingredients together to form a dough. Turn out onto a floured surface and knead the dough lightly until smooth.

Divide the dough into 4 equal portions and pat each piece into a round shape about 18cm (7in) in diameter and 1cm (½in) thick. Place the dough rounds onto a lightly greased baking tray and top with the mixture of your choice. Bake in the oven for 15–20 minutes or until cooked and golden brown on top. Serve.

POLENTA PIZZA CRUST

Although this no-dough pizza base does not need to rise, it does need to dry, so it is a good idea to make it in the morning and finish it off in the evening.

SERVES 4 AS A STARTER AND 2 AS A MAIN COURSE

450ml (16fl oz) vegetable stock
175g (6oz) polenta or maize meal
1 teaspoon salt
55g (2oz) parmesan cheese, grated
1 egg, beaten
olive oil, for brushing

Bring the stock to the boil in a saucepan. Place the polenta or maize meal and salt in a bowl and stir to mix. Keeping the pan of boiling stock at a rolling boil, stir the polenta or maize meal mixture into the boiling stock and continue to simmer, stirring vigorously, for about 5 minutes, or until the mixture is thick. Remove the pan from the heat and stir in the parmesan.

Place the egg in a bowl, add a spoonful of the hot polenta and beat until well mixed,

PYREX

then add the egg mixture to the polenta in the pan and beat for a further minute or so. Set aside and leave to cool.

Grease a 23cm (9in) round or square baking sheet and form the cooled polenta into a crust about 1cm (½in) thick on the baking sheet. Do this by patting it into shape using wet hands – needless to say, children like to do this part! Leave the pizza crust to stand for several hours until it is fairly dry.

Preheat the oven to 180°C/350°F/Gas Mark 4. Brush the top of the polenta crust with oil, then bake in the oven for 45–60 minutes or until dry and crisp, brushing the surface of the polenta crust with oil every 15 minutes. Top the polenta crust with your favourite topping and bake for a further 5–10 minutes, or until cooked. Serve.

SCONE PIZZA BASE

This is the base I make most often and one we use a lot for pizzas in our shops. It has a nice soft, flaky texture and holds the toppings beautifully.

SERVES 4

- 225g (8oz) wholemeal or white self-raising flour (mix half-and-half if you like)
- ½ teaspoon baking powder
- 55g (2oz) butter
- 2 eggs
- about 2 tablespoons milk
- ½ teaspoon mixed dried herbs
- ½ teaspoon mustard powder
- salt and freshly ground black pepper
- olive oil, for brushing

Preheat the oven to 200°C/400°F/Gas Mark 6. Place the flour and baking powder in a bowl and lightly rub the butter into the flour until the mixture resembles breadcrumbs.

Beat the eggs and milk together and add to the flour mixture with the herbs, mustard powder and seasoning. Stir together using your hands until the mixture begins to stick together, adding a little extra milk,

Left: A rich organic tomato sauce will go beautifully under most toppings. Why not make a good quantity and freeze some for next time?

if necessary. Collect the dough together to form a ball of soft dough and knead lightly.

Press the dough evenly over the base of a 25cm (10in) pizza dish or shallow, round baking tin. Brush the top of the dough with oil and bake in the oven for 15 minutes. Top the dough with Fast Fresh Tomato Sauce (see recipe on page 102), followed by the topping of your choice and bake for a further 5–10 minutes, or until the pizza is cooked and golden brown. Serve.

mix and match pizza toppings

If you are making pizza bases at the last minute, you will probably invent combinations from whatever you have to hand. The combinations given here are intended as guides to flavours that go well together.

FAST FRESH TOMATO SAUCE

A tomato sauce base is the classic topping to go under other things, but it is not imperative.

SERVES 4

450g (1lb) tomatoes, skinned, deseeded and chopped, or 400g (14oz) can chopped tomatoes
2 cloves garlic, crushed
2 teaspoons sugar
1 teaspoon dried oregano
½ teaspoon salt
½ teaspoon freshly ground black pepper

Place all the ingredients in a saucepan, stir to mix, then bring to the boil. Reduce the heat and simmer, uncovered, for about 30 minutes, stirring occasionally. Use as required.

NAPOLITANA

SERVES 4

Sauté 1 thinly sliced red onion and 2 cloves of finely chopped garlic in a little olive oil until softened. Spread the chosen pizza dough with a thin layer of tomato sauce, then top with the sautéed onion and garlic, 5 chopped anchovy fillets, 8 halved and stoned black olives, four 125g (4½oz) whole mozzarella, thinly sliced, and 1 teaspoon drained capers. Drizzle with 4 tablespoons olive oil, sprinkle with chopped fresh oregano and bake in the oven as directed.

MUSHROOM, RICOTTA AND OLIVES

SERVES 4

Thinly slice 115g (4oz) mushrooms and sauté them in a little olive oil until softened. Spread the chosen pizza dough with tomato sauce and spoon mushrooms over this. Top with small scoops taken from 115g (4oz) ricotta cheese and top the cheese with 8 thinly sliced pitted black olives. Sprinkle with chopped fresh thyme and rosemary and drizzle with olive oil. Bake in the oven as directed.

Left: You can use almost anything you like to top a pizza – choose the freshest organic ingredients you can find

MOZZARELLA, ONIONS AND GREEN PEPPER

SERVES 4

Heat 1 tablespoon olive oil in a frying pan, add 55g (2oz) thinly sliced onions and 55g (2oz) finely chopped, deseeded green pepper and sauté until soft. Stir in a few pinches of chopped fresh oregano and freshly ground black pepper. Spread tomato sauce over a pre-baked polenta pizza crust and top with the onion and peppers.

Preheat the grill to medium. Crumble 175g (6oz) mozzarella cheese and scatter two-thirds of it over the pizza. Top with tomato slices and the remaining mozzarella. Sprinkle a little parmesan cheese over the top. Place the pizza under the grill until the cheese is melted and lightly browned. Serve.

SPICY SAUSAGE AND POTATO

SERVES 4

Choose a spicy cured sausage (about 115g/4oz) for this topping and cut it into thin slices, or buy pre-sliced cured sausage. Boil, drain and peel 2 large or 4 small potatoes, then slice them into 3mm (⅛in) thick slices.

Preheat the oven to 180°C/350°F/Gas Mark 4 or preheat the grill to medium. Sauté the potato slices in a little olive oil with some salt and freshly ground black pepper for about 3–4 minutes, or until golden. Spread the chosen pre-cooked pizza base with tomato sauce, then place the potatoe slices on top. Place the sausage slices on top of the potatoes and bake or grill until cooked and golden.

BACON AND ONION

SERVES 4

This is particularly good with the potato pizzetta. Sauté 1 thinly sliced large onion in olive oil until soft and golden. Meanwhile, cook 115g (4oz) lean back bacon rashers until done and just starting to crisp, turning occasionally, then snip into small pieces. Spoon the onions over the pizzetta pizza bases and top with the bacon. Bake in the oven as directed. Serve.

Right: Spicy sausage and potato and (far right) bacon and onion toppings

stir-fries

This is a wonderful way to use the contents of your organic vegetable box, because virtually all vegetables stir-fry beautifully.

BASIC STIR-FRY

SERVES 4

225g (8oz) short grain brown rice
salt and freshly ground black pepper
2 tablespoons olive or sesame oil
2 cloves garlic, crushed
1cm (½in) piece fresh root ginger, peeled and grated
1 onion, finely chopped, or 2 leeks, washed and cut into matchsticks
about 450g (1lb) prepared mixed fresh vegetables, finely chopped or sliced (choose from carrots, peppers, cabbage, broccoli, kohlrabi, celery, beansprouts, mangetout are all suitable, but avoid potato, beetroot, turnip and swede)
2 tablespoons soya sauce

Place the rice and 1 teaspoon salt in a large saucepan and add 700ml (1¼ pints) water. Bring to the boil, then reduce the heat, cover with a tight-fitting lid and simmer for about 40 minutes, or until all the water has been absorbed and the rice is tender.

Heat the oil in a wok, add the garlic and ginger and stir-fry over a high heat, until they begin to brown. Add the onion or leeks and stir-fry until softened, then add the remaining prepared vegetables and stir-fry for about 2–3 minutes or until cooked to your liking.

Add the hot cooked rice and soya sauce and stir-fry to mix. Season with salt and pepper.

SPICY

SERVES 4

Follow the ingredients and method for the Basic Stir-fry recipe and when you add the prepared vegetables to the wok, also add 2 small deseeded and finely chopped fresh red chillies, 2 tablespoons chopped fresh coriander and 1 teaspoon crushed cardamom seeds.

ORIENTAL

SERVES 4

Follow the ingredients and method for the Basic Stir-fry recipe but instead of adding the soya sauce, mix together the following ingredients and add to the wok with the rice: 4 tablespoons soya sauce, 1 tablespoon cider vinegar, 1 tablespoon dry sherry, 1 tablespoon sugar, 1 tablespoon grated fresh root ginger and 225g (8oz) shelled cashew nuts (optional).

MEDITERRANEAN

SERVES 4

Follow the ingredients and method for the Basic Stir-fry recipe, but add a few strands of saffron and 1 teaspoon turmeric when you cook the garlic and ginger, and add 115g (4oz) raw peeled prawns when you add the prepared vegetables.

Opposite: Basic Stir-Fry, mix stir-fried vegetables with brown rice – the tastes and textures of this dish are habit-forming
Left: Possible variations are almost endless, as shown by the ingredients for (from top) Spicy, Oriental and Mediterranean combinations

one-pot suppers

The take on these dishes is that all your meal is in one pot and you don't have to do anything else once the pot is prepared – except serve it! Weekday meals need to be like this.

COCONUT CHICKEN WITH SWEET POTATOES AND BUTTERNUT SQUASH

Add a chilli if serving this to adults, but be careful if it is for children – you could have a sleepless night! The lime leaves are also optional as they are an acquired taste – I love them, but again children might not.

SERVES 4

- 55g (2oz) butter
- 2 tablespoons olive oil
- 1 onion, finely chopped
- 1 clove garlic, crushed
- 1 fresh red chilli, deseeded and finely chopped (optional)
- 8 medium portions of chicken, skinned (about 1kg/2¼lb in total weight)
- 450ml (16fl oz) chicken or vegetable stock
- 4 lime leaves, fresh or frozen (defrosted), chopped (optional)
- 450g (1lb) sweet potatoes, cut into 2.5cm (1in) cubes
- 450g (1lb) butternut squash or another yellow squash, peeled and cut into 2.5cm (1in) cubes
- 350ml (12fl oz) coconut milk
- 1 tablespoon finely chopped fresh coriander
- salt and freshly ground black pepper

Heat the butter and oil in a heavy-based saucepan until the butter is melted. Add the onion, garlic and chilli, if using, and sauté until they are softened and turning brown, stirring occasionally.

Add the chicken portions and cook until sealed on both sides, turning occasionally. Add the stock and lime leaves, if using, then bring to the boil, cover and simmer for about 30 minutes, or until the chicken is cooked and tender. Add the sweet potatoes, squash and coconut milk and stir to mix. Reduce the heat to low, cover and cook gently for about 10 minutes or until the potatoes and squash are tender – do not let the coconut milk boil, as it will separate. Stir in the chopped coriander and season to taste with salt and pepper. Serve with cooked rice and fresh greens, if liked.

FRAGRANT PORK AND APRICOT CASSEROLE

Organic pork comes from a far happier pig and you can read why on page 16. Start this dish the afternoon or evening before you want to cook it, as the pork is marinated for 24 hours before the cooking begins.

SERVES 4

- 900g (2lb) lean boneless pork, cut into 2.5cm (1in) pieces
- 8 ready-to-eat dried apricots, cut into quarters
- 115g (4oz) sultanas
- 225ml (8fl oz) red wine
- 125ml (4fl oz) cider vinegar
- 1 teaspoon ground cumin
- 1 teaspoon ground coriander
- 1 teaspoon salt
- 1 teaspoon freshly ground black pepper
- 2 tablespoons olive oil
- 2 onions, sliced
- 2 cloves garlic, crushed
- 600ml (1 pint) chicken or vegetable stock
- 2 tablespoons runny honey
- 2 bay leaves

Opposite: Coconut Chicken with Sweet Potatoes and Butternut Squash

Place the pork, apricots and sultanas in a non-metallic dish. Mix together the wine, vinegar, ground spices and salt and pepper and pour over the pork mixture. Stir to mix well. Cover and leave to marinate in the refrigerator for 24 hours.

When you are ready to cook the casserole, preheat the oven to 180°C/350°F/Gas Mark 4. Remove the pork from the marinade using a slotted spoon, pat it dry on absorbent kitchen paper and place it in a dish. Remove the fruit from the marinade, place on a plate and set aside. Reserve the marinade. Heat the oil in a frying pan, add the pork, a few pieces at a time, and sauté until browned all over, stirring occasionally. Place the pork in a large, flameproof, ovenproof casserole dish and set aside. Sauté the remaining pork in batches until it is all browned.

Sauté the onions and garlic in the same frying pan for 5 minutes, stirring occasionally, then add the reserved marinade and scrape the pan to add to the juices. Cook for several minutes, until slightly reduced, stirring occasionally. Add to the casserole with the reserved fruit, the stock, honey and bay leaves and stir to mix. Bring to the boil on the hob, then cover and bake in the oven for 1 hour, stirring occasionally. Stir in a little more hot stock or wine if the meat seems too dry, then return the casserole to the oven, uncovered, and bake for a further 30 minutes, or until the pork is cooked and tender. Remove and discard the bay leaves. Serve with cooked rice and green vegetables.

MOUSSAKA OF SQUASH WITH FETA CHEESE TOPPING

Use either squash or marrow – preferably baby marrows – for this dish.

SERVES 4

3 tablespoons olive oil
1 onion, chopped
900g (2lb) any type of squash (a mixture is good), peeled and chopped
2 cloves garlic, finely chopped
one 400g (14oz) can chopped tomatoes
1 tablespoon tomato purée
2 tablespoons vegeatble bouillon powder (optional)
1 tablespoon finely chopped fresh parsley
salt and freshly ground black pepper
2 eggs, lightly beaten
90ml (3fl oz) milk
90ml (3fl oz) crême fraiche
½ teaspoon grated nutmeg
225g (8oz) feta cheese, crumbled
chopped fresh parsley, to garnish

Preheat the oven to 190°C/375°F/Gas Mark 5. Heat the oil in a frying pan, add the onion and sauté until soft, stirring occasionally. Add the squash and garlic, stir to mix, then cook for 1 minute. Add the tomatoes and cook for a further 10 minutes, stirring occasionally. Stir in the tomato purée and season with salt and pepper.

Spoon the mixture into an ovenproof casserole dish, leaving room for the topping. Whisk the eggs with the milk, crême fraiche and nutmeg, stir in the feta cheese and season to taste with salt and pepper. Pour the cheese mixture evenly over the squash mixture in the dish. Bake in the oven for about 30 minutes or until cooked and golden brown. Garnish with parsley and serve with salad.

RICOTTA AND VEGETABLE NOODLE BAKE

SERVES 4–6

85g (3oz) butter, plus extra for greasing
1 large onion, chopped
2 stalks broccoli, broken into small florets and stems thinly sliced
450g (1lb) mushrooms, thinly sliced
225g (8oz) fresh spinach leaves, washed and torn into small pieces
350g (12oz) fresh or dried flat egg noodles
salt and freshly ground black pepper
3 eggs

Right: A mixture of squash or marrow makes a rich, warming Moussaka

700g (1lb 9oz) ricotta cheese
225ml (8fl oz) sour cream
125ml (4fl oz) dry white wine
55g (2oz) fresh breadcrumbs or wheatgerm
115g (4oz) cheddar or parmesan cheese, grated

Preheat the oven to 180°C/350°F/Gas Mark 4. Grease a 23x33cm (9x13in) ovenproof dish with a little butter and set aside. Melt the remaining butter in a heavy-based frying pan, add the onion and sauté until soft, stirring occasionally. Add the broccoli, mushrooms and spinach and sauté for about 5 minutes or until the vegetables are all soft, stirring occasionally.

Meanwhile, cook the noodles in a saucepan of lightly salted, boiling water for about 5 minutes for fresh noodles or 10 minutes for dried noodles, or until tender but firm. Drain well. Break the eggs into a large bowl and beat lightly, then whisk in the ricotta and sour cream until well mixed. Add the sautéed vegetables, noodles and wine and mix well.

Turn the mixture into the prepared dish and spread it out evenly. Mix the breadcrumbs or wheatgerm and cheese together and sprinkle over the top of the vegetable mixture. Cover and bake in the oven for 30 minutes, then uncover and bake for a further 15 minutes, until golden brown on top. Serve.

family feasts

Meals should be shared occasions, because nothing holds a family together so much as the shared ritual of eating and talking together at meal times.

Of course, our notion of family has been stretched in recent years and can now mean the extended family in all its many modern forms. But what matters most is that a close group of people behave in a loving and supportive way to one another. And nothing strengthens these bonds between family members more than formal meals eaten in traditional fashion around the dinner table.

This often means a lot of work for one or two people, but the cooking can be rotated among several adults. Try to include children and young people in the preparations, too – that's part of the fun. But the centrepiece is, of course, the meal itself, when young and old sit around a table and talk together.

Rituals such as polishing silver, folding napkins or setting out glasses can be accompanied by stories of how these items came into the family's possession. We all have simple stories of this kind – and they all serve to enrich the child's experience and increase and enhance their sense of belonging.

I'm a great believer, too, in taking children to visit old houses to explore their kitchens and kitchen gardens. In this way, children learn about the way things used to be, the importance of the seasons – still applicable to organic farming – and the way people's lives were shaped by these in the past.

They will also learn and appreciate the central role of family meals where people eat good, wholesome food prepared at home and experience all the elements of the meal-time ritual: good manners, conversation, and all the pleasures of loving and friendly company. Can anything be more important?

Bio

weekend roasts

Even the phrase 'Sunday joint' sounds quaint and old-fashioned now. It probably means something quite different to the younger generation, too! But I like the idea of a roast joint as a family dinner on Sunday. It's an English tradition and I'm all in favour of preserving it.

The only difficulty lies in finding someone who can carve a joint properly! So, make sure you train up at least one member of the family – and give them a 'carver's perk', in the shape of a glass of wine or beer, to keep them sweet.

A leg of lamb, roasted with rosemary and garlic, is my all-time favourite Sunday choice. For the full Monty, serve it with roast potatoes, parsnips and onions, honey-glazed carrots, field mushrooms sautéed in butter, garlic, parsley and Worcestershire sauce, red wine gravy, and redcurrant and mint jelly!

Or, choose game in season – this could be pheasant, partridge, wood pigeon, venison or grouse. Simply roast in a hot oven, following the butcher's instructions, and serve with Brussels sprouts, home-made Oven Chips, Bread Sauce, and a thick Red Wine and Berry Jam Gravy (see recipes on pages 90, 124 and 122).

It's a personal decision, but if you prefer your potatoes crisp, roast them in a separate tin at the top of the oven. Allow 50ml (2fl oz) olive oil per 450g (1lb) potatoes and heat the oil before adding the potatoes.

LEG OF LAMB PAN-ROASTED WITH POTATOES, PARSNIPS AND ONIONS

If you don't want all the vegetables, just roast the lamb on its own in the same way with the garlic and rosemary. Potatoes roasted with the meat will not be as crisp as if they were roasted on their own, but they will pick up all the juices of the meat and so have a wonderful flavour.

SERVES 6

1 leg of lamb, weighing 2–2.5kg (4½–5½lb)
6 cloves juicy garlic, sliced lengthways (about 8 slices per clove)
4 bushy sprigs fresh rosemary, broken into tiny sprigs
2 tablespoons olive oil
2 teaspoons coarse salt
12 medium potatoes, halved or quartered
salt and freshly ground black pepper
3 large or 6 small Spanish onions, quartered or halved
6 parsnips, each cut into 4 strips
300ml (½ pint) red or white wine (depending on the wine you will be drinking with the meal)

Preheat the oven to 230°C/450°F/Gas Mark 8. Place the lamb in a flameproof roasting tin, cut slits through the skin of the lamb all over the top using a sharp knife, then push one piece of garlic and one sprig of rosemary into each slit. Turn the lamb over and do the same on the underside. Turn back so that the top side is facing up and rub 1 tablespoon oil all over the lamb, followed by the salt.

Roast the lamb in the oven for 30 minutes, then reduce the oven temperature to 180°C/350°F/Gas Mark 4 and roast the lamb for a further 2 hours, basting from time to time with the juices. If you like your meat rare, reduce the cooking time by 30 minutes or so. If you like your meat well done, you may need to increase the cooking time by about 15–30 minutes.

Meanwhile, place the potatoes in a saucepan of lightly salted water, bring to the boil and boil for about 3 minutes. Drain well. About 45 minutes before the lamb is ready, withdraw the roasting tin from the oven and arrange the potatoes, onions and parsnips around the meat and drizzle the remaining oil over them. Sprinkle with salt and freshly ground black pepper, then return to the oven and continue to roast, turning the vegetables and basting the meat once or twice.

When the meat is cooked, place it on a warm serving dish and allow it to relax for 15 minutes before serving.

Place the vegetables on another dish and keep warm, while you make the gravy.

There won't be much fat or many juices left as the vegetables will have soaked these up, so scrape the meaty and crusty bits off the bottom and sides of the tin with a wooden spoon. Pour in the wine, bring to the boil, then reduce the heat and simmer until the liquid has reduced to about two-thirds of its original volume, stirring occasionally.

Season to taste, then pour into a gravy boat. If you would like a more substantial, thicker gravy, follow the instructions for making the gravy in the Roast Saddle of Lamb recipe on page 152. Carve the lamb and serve with the vegetables and gravy.

THYME AND LEMON ROAST CHICKEN

Chicken was a very special dish for us wartime children when meat was strictly rationed. My husband remembers eating chicken once a year at Christmas. I was one of the lucky ones: my mother kept a small flock of hens in the garden of our south London home, and every month my father would catch, dispatch and pluck one for a special Sunday roast. My mother usually stuffed it with the traditional mixture of sage and onions bound with breadcrumbs and a little milk – things that were easy to lay your hands on in wartime or the post-war years of austerity.

Not surprisingly, I'm less keen on sage and onion stuffing now and prefer richer mixtures. I'm much more liberal with the use of butter, too – but in wartime, of course, butter also was strictly rationed and the use of two ounces of this precious fat to roast a chicken would have shocked my mother deeply. Butter is not essential here, though. You can use olive oil if you prefer, to give a different but equally delicious flavour. For a special occasion, try one of the more exotic stuffings on pages 120–122.

SERVES 4

1.8kg (4lb) oven-ready chicken
115g (4oz) butter
2 cloves garlic, crushed
salt and freshly ground black pepper
1 tablespoon finely chopped fresh thyme
1 lemon, sliced
2 bay leaves
300ml (½ pint) chicken stock or half stock and half dry or medium white wine
plain flour, for sprinkling (optional)

Preheat the oven to 200°C/400°F/Gas Mark 6. Wash and dry the chicken, then place it in a shallow roasting tin.

Mix 55g (2oz) butter with the garlic and seasoning and rub this mixture all over the bird. Mix the remaining butter with the thyme and press this mixture into the neck end and lower end of the bird, dividing it equally between the two. Place the lemon slices and bay leaves inside the bird after the thyme mixture. Tuck the neck skin under.

Roast in the oven for about 1½ hours, basting with the juices occasionally. Place a piece of greaseproof paper over the breast when the breast skin starts to brown.

Remove the greaseproof paper, baste the chicken well, then roast it for a further 15 minutes, or until cooked and tender. Place the cooked chicken on a plate and keep hot, while you make the gravy.

For a thin gravy, pour off all the fat from the meat juices, leaving behind the sediment. Season with salt and pepper and add the hot stock or stock and wine. Bring to the boil, stirring. Carve the chicken and serve with the gravy.

If you like a thicker gravy, once again pour off all the fat, leaving about 2 tablespoons juices and sediment in the tin. Sprinkle a little flour over the juices and whisk over a high heat until combined. Whisk in the hot stock or stock and wine and bring to the boil, whisking, until the gravy thickens. Simmer for 2–3 minutes, stirring. Season to taste with salt and pepper. Carve the chicken and serve with the gravy.

CINNAMON-SPICED ROAST PORK WITH CIDER AND APPLE GRAVY

Choose a fillet end of leg of pork, which gives you lots of lean meat and crunchy crackling.

This joint is best bought a day or two before cooking and then left uncovered in the bottom of the refrigerator to dry, as this will help to produce a really crisp crackling.

Roast the pork with a little apple-derived alcohol such as calvados or dry or medium cider and some chopped apple as well. Pork and apple is a heady mix and cinnamon adds a delightful fragrance. For a serious feast, serve with Stuffed Apples (see recipe on page 64).

SERVES 6

1 joint of leg of pork, weighing 2–2.5kg (4½–5½lb)
4 teaspoons ground cinnamon
salt and freshly ground black pepper
1 tablespoon olive oil
2 cooking apples, peeled, cored and chopped
1 tablespoon plain flour

300ml (½ pint) dry or medium cider, or 150ml (¼ pint) calvados plus an extra 150ml (¼ pint) stock
300ml (½ pint) vegetable stock (or vegetable bouillon powder dissolved in boiling water)

Preheat the oven to 240°C/475°F/Gas Mark 9. Score the skin of the pork with a sharp paring knife, going right down into the fat that lies under the skin. Ask your butcher to show you how to do this if you are unsure. If it is already scored, do a few more for good measure.

Place the pork, skin side up, on a rack in a heavy-based roasting tin. Mix the cinnamon with 4 teaspoons salt and the oil and rub this mixture evenly over the skin, pressing it in as you go. Place the pork on the highest shelf in the oven and roast for 25 minutes.

Take the tin out of the oven and place the chopped apples in the bottom of the tin. Reduce the oven temperature to 190°C/375°F/Gas Mark 5. Return to the oven and roast for a further 2¾–3½ hours or until the pork is cooked (insert a skewer into the thickest part of the meat – the juices should run clear when the meat is cooked). Remove from the oven and leave to stand for about 30 minutes – this allows the meat to relax and makes it more tender.

Meanwhile, make the gravy. Tilt the roasting tin and remove the fat with a spoon, or if the juices are very fatty pour them (without the apples) into a measuring jug and put in a cool place until the fat separates (in this case, keep the joint warm), then return the juices to the tin.

Sprinkle the flour onto the remaining juices in the tin and, over a low heat, work the flour into the juices using a wooden spoon and crushing the apples as you go. Increase the heat and gently whisk everything together while you gradually pour in the cider or calvados and stock. Continue whisking and heating the gravy until it comes to the boil. Simmer for 2–3 minutes, stirring. Season to taste with salt and pepper, then pour the gravy into a serving jug.

Carve the pork in thick slices and serve with a piece of crackling. Pour some gravy over the meat and hand the rest around in a jug at the table. Ring the changes on roast potatoes by serving this pork with a creamy mash of potatoes and parsnips. Use 2 potatoes of every parsnip.

For a festive occasion, omit the apples and serve with Stuffed Apples (see recipe on page 64).

ROAST GOOSE WITH FRESH CHESTNUT STUFFING

Goose has a dark and flavourful meat and is becoming increasingly popular as a substitute for turkey. Traditionally stuffed with fresh chestnuts, the combination is extremely successful.

SERVES 6

2.25kg (5lb) oven-ready goose (prepared for the oven by your butcher)
salt
450g (1lb) Chestnut Stuffing (see page 120)

Preheat the oven to 200°C/400°F/Gas Mark 6. Prick the skin of the goose all over with a sharp fork to allow the fat to escape, then sprinkle the bird with salt and stuff with the chestnut stuffing. Place it on a rack in a roasting tin – you must always use a rack or the goose will fry in its own fat. Smear the goose all over with the fat taken from the inside of the goose and cover the bird with greaseproof paper.

Roast the goose in the oven for 1½–1¾ hours. Remove the greaseproof paper for the last 30 minutes of the cooking time to allow the skin to brown. Test that the goose is cooked by inserting a sharp knife at the point where the leg meets the body. Cut the flesh slightly – if the meat is not red, the goose is cooked. Place the goose on a warm serving plate and keep warm while making the gravy.

To make the gravy, spoon the fat off and make a gravy with stock or red wine – follow the recipe for Red Wine and Berry Jam Gravy (see page 122) but omit the jam.

Carve the meat and serve with the stuffing, the gravy and Braised Sweet and Sour Red Cabbage (see page 119).

vegetarian roasts

MUSHROOM AND CARROT LOAF

This unusual vegetable bake is great served with a fragrant Ginger and Cashew nut sauce (see recipe on page 124).

SERVES 4

115g (4oz) butter or non-hydrogenated vegetable margarine, plus extra for greasing
1 onion, finely chopped
2 cloves garlic, crushed
225g (8oz) mushrooms, chopped
175g (6oz) fresh breadcrumbs
115g (4oz) cheddar cheese (or vegan cheese), grated
225g (8oz) carrots, coarsely grated
2 eggs, beaten (or soya milk for vegans), to bind
1 teaspoon dried thyme
1 teaspoon dried basil
salt and freshly ground black pepper

Preheat the oven to 180°C/350°F/Gas Mark 4. Grease a 900g (2lb) loaf tin with a little butter or margarine and set aside. Melt 55g (2oz) butter or margarine in a saucepan, add the onion and sauté until soft, stirring occasionally. Add the garlic and mushrooms and sauté until soft, stirring occasionally. Remove the pan from the heat.

Reserve half the breadcrumbs and half the cheese and set aside. Add the remaining breadcrumbs and cheese to the onion mixture together with the carrots, eggs (or milk), dried herbs and seasoning and mix well.

Spoon the mixture into the prepared tin and level the surface. Mix the reserved breadcrumbs and cheese together and sprinkle over the top, then dot with the remaining butter or margarine. Cover with greaseproof paper and bake in the oven for 30 minutes. Remove the paper and bake for a further 5 minutes or until browned.

Turn out onto a warmed serving plate and serve in slices with Ginger and Cashew Nut Sauce (see page 124).

BRAZIL NUT ROAST

This is a beautifully simple recipe which we make at the restaurant every Christmas and serve with a cranberry and red wine gravy.

SERVES 4

25g (1oz) butter, plus extra for greasing
350g (12oz) brazil nuts
55g (2oz) onions, finely chopped
55g (2oz) carrots, finely chopped
55g (2oz) celery, finely chopped
175g (6oz) fresh breadcrumbs
2 tablespoons finely chopped fresh parsley
1 tablespoon dried mixed herbs
salt and freshly ground black pepper
2 eggs, beaten
about 125ml (4fl oz) vegetable stock

Preheat the oven to 200°C/400°F/Gas Mark 6. Grease a 900g (2lb) loaf tin with a little butter and set aside. Chop the nuts finely – you will need a food processor or a pestle and mortar to do this – then set aside. Melt the remaining 25g (1oz) butter in a saucepan, add the onions, carrots and celery and sauté for 5 minutes, stirring occasionally.

Place the sautéed vegetables, chopped nuts, breadcrumbs, fresh and dried herbs, and salt and pepper in a bowl and stir to mix. Stir in the beaten eggs, then add enough stock to bind the mixture together – the mixture should be quite sticky and moist but not wet.

Spoon into the prepared tin and level the surface. Bake for about 30 minutes or until cooked and lightly browned. Turn out onto a serving plate and serve in slices with Red Wine and Berry Jam Gravy (see page 122).

Opposite: Nut roasts may not be original but I think they're hard to beat as a vegetarian alternative to roast meat.

vegetables for roasts

Most people have their favourite vegetables, and if you are using organic ingredients you don't need to do anything fancy as the flavours are so wonderful. If you feel like doing something different, however, here are some ideas. Remember that it's a good idea to buy seasonal vegetables, as they will be the freshest and full of flavour.

RATATOUILLE

SERVES 4

- 1 large aubergine, sliced
- salt and freshly ground black pepper
- 2 tablespoons olive oil
- 2 onions, roughly chopped
- 2 cloves garlic, crushed
- 2 courgettes, sliced
- 1 small red pepper, deseeded and roughly chopped
- 400g (14oz) can chopped tomatoes
- 1 bay leaf

Place the aubergine slices in a colander with a sprinkling of salt between each layer, then place a plate on top and weigh it down. Set aside for 30 minutes. Rinse the aubergines thoroughly under cold water, then pat dry with absorbent kitchen paper.

Heat the oil in a saucepan, add the onions and sauté until they are soft and browning slightly, stirring occasionally. Add the garlic, courgettes, red pepper, aubergines, tomatoes, bay leaf and seasoning and stir to mix. Cover and simmer for about 30 minutes, or until the vegetables are cooked and tender, stirring occasionally. Discard the bay leaf and serve.

JERUSALEM ARTICHOKES

I adore these unusual roots. You can brighten up a dull meal by serving them in lemon cream, as here, or purée them to serve with a roast meat or nut roast. The main thing is to peel the artichokes well and boil them for about 10 minutes with a slice of lemon juice, which stops the roots discolouring. Then, either drain and sauté them in a little butter and lemon juice for a further 5 minutes, or mash the cooked artichokes before adding cream, seasoning and a pinch of ground nutmeg.

SERVES 4

- 700g (1lb 9oz) Jerusalem artichokes, cut into chunks
- 1 lemon, cut in half and juiced, reserving a slice for cooking
- salt and freshly ground black pepper
- 55g (2oz) butter
- 150ml (¼ pint) single cream
- a pinch of ground nutmeg

Place the artichokes in a saucepan with a slice of lemon. Cover with lightly salted, cold water, then cover and bring to the boil. Simmer for about 10 minutes or until cooked and tender, then drain well and set aside.

Melt the butter in a separate saucepan, add the artichokes and lemon juice, cover and cook for a further 8 minutes, shaking the pan occasionally. Remove the pan from the heat and stir in the cream, nutmeg and seasoning. Heat gently until hot, stirring occasionally. Serve.

CARROTS GLAZED WITH HONEY AND NUTMEG

If you prefer, you can leave the nutmeg out of this recipe.

SERVES 4

- 700g (1lb 9oz) carrots
- salt and freshly ground black pepper
- 55g (2oz) butter
- 2 tablespoons runny honey
- 2 teaspoons ground nutmeg

Scrub the carrots. If they are new and very small, you can leave them whole; otherwise, cut them into long strips.

Cook the carrots in a saucepan of lightly salted, boiling water for 5–10 minutes, depending on their size, until just tender but not soft. Drain well.

Melt the butter in a frying pan, add the carrots and sauté until *al dente*, stirring occasionally. Stir in the honey and nutmeg and season to taste with salt and pepper. Reheat gently, then serve.

BALSAMIC ROASTED ROOT VEGETABLES

People are sometimes perplexed by what to do with rootie things that turn up in their organic veggie boxes – like fennel and celeriac, or even beetroot. A good idea is to half cook them in boiling water and then finish by roasting them in the oven with balsamic vinegar.

Preheat the oven to 230°C/450°F/Gas Mark 8. Trim your vegetables, removing and discarding any tough outer layers. Cut the vegetables into smallish pieces, about 5cm (2in) in diameter or square, then cook them in a saucepan of lightly salted, boiling water for about 15–30 minutes depending on the root. When tender but still firm, drain well and place in a baking tin.

Drizzle a little olive oil all over the vegetables, sprinkle with salt and toss to coat them all over. Roast in the oven for about 20 minutes, then reduce the oven temperature to 190°C/375°F/Gas Mark 5, drizzle some balsamic vinegar over the vegetables and roast in the oven for a further 10 minutes. Serve.

BRAISED SWEET AND SOUR RED CABBAGE

SERVES 4

900g (2lb) red cabbage, shredded
2 onions, sliced
2 cooking apples, peeled, cored and chopped
2 teaspoons sugar
salt and freshly ground black pepper
1 fresh bouquet garni made using 1 bay leaf, sprig of fresh thyme, sprig of fresh sage and sprig of fresh rosemary
2 tablespoons red wine vinegar
25g (1oz) butter

Preheat the oven to 170°C/325°F/Gas Mark 3. Layer the cabbage in a casserole dish with the onions, apples, sugar and seasoning. Make a well in the middle and place the bouquet garni in the well. Spoon over the vinegar and 2 tablespoons water. Cover and bake in the oven for about 2 hours or until fragrant and tender, stirring occasionally. Discard the bouquet garni. Stir well and dot with butter before serving.

MUSHROOMS

SERVES 4

This method, known as Bordelaise, combines the taste of the mushrooms with parsley and garlic – a magic combination. Simply wipe 700g (1lb 9oz) mushrooms, cut them into slices and sauté them in 1 tablespoon oil and 25g (1oz) melted butter with 1 chopped shallot, 1 clove crushed garlic, 1 tablespoon finely chopped fresh parsley and salt and freshly ground black pepper for about 5 minutes. I stir in 1 tablespoon Worcestershire sauce just before turning off the heat. Serve.

CARAMELIZED ONIONS

SERVES 4–6

1 tablespoon olive oil
25g (1oz) butter
2 large onions, each cut lengthways into 8 wedges
2 cloves garlic, thinly sliced

Heat the oil and butter in a shallow pan until the butter is melted. Add the onions and garlic and cook gently for about 20 minutes, or until the onions are soft and golden brown, stirring occasionally. Watch the onions carefully and make sure they don't burn. Serve.

stuffings and sauces

The finishing touches of gravy and stuffing are so easy that it is really worth spending that little bit of extra time on them. They can turn a mundane meal into a corker.

APRICOT AND WALNUT STUFFING

This goes well with poultry such as chicken, turkey and guinea fowl.

SERVES 4–6

- 85g (3oz) dried apricots
- 25g (1oz) sultanas
- 150ml (¼ pint) fortified wine such as sherry, port or madeira
- 85g (3oz) fresh breadcrumbs
- 25g (1oz) walnuts, finely chopped
- 25g (1oz) butter, softened
- 1 tablespoon lemon juice
- 1 teaspoon finely grated lemon zest
- 1 teaspoon ground mixed spice
- ¼ teaspoon salt
- ¼ teaspoon freshly ground black pepper
- 1 egg, beaten

Place the apricots and sultanas in a bowl, pour over the fortified wine and stir to mix. Leave to soak overnight. Drain the fruit, reserving the fortified wine, then finely chop the fruit. Place the chopped fruit in a bowl, add the reserved wine and all the remaining ingredients and mix thoroughly. Either use this mixture to stuff the cavity of the chicken at the beginning of cooking, or cook the stuffing in a small ovenproof dish alongside the chicken for the last 30 minutes of the roasting time. If you cook the stuffing separately it will be crisper.

Opposite: Tangy Fruit Stuffing is substantial enough to be eaten on its own

TANGY FRUIT STUFFING

This stuffing from Iran uses barberries, which once grew prolifically in England, and were found in many recipes from medieval times up until the last century. Although too sour to eat on their own, they give a refreshing tartness when mixed with sweeter fruit. As a variation, use dried cranberries.

SERVES 4–6

- 8 ready-to-eat dried peaches, cut into quarters
- 4 dessertspoons dried barberries or cranberries
- 6 dessertspoons dried cherries
- 1 tablespoon olive oil
- 25g (1oz) butter
- 2 onions, chopped
- 2 dessertspoons coarsely chopped walnuts
- 4 dessertspoons tomato purée
- salt, to taste

Wash and dry all the dried fruit and set aside. Heat the oil and butter in a frying pan until the butter is melted, add the onions and sauté until soft and golden, stirring occasionally. Stir in the walnuts and dried fruit and cook for a further 1 minute, stirring. Stir in the tomato purée and salt to taste and mix well. Use as required, or finish cooking in the oven in a baking tin for 5 minutes and serve as part of a vegetarian meal instead of the meat.

CHESTNUT STUFFING

Good for roast goose or duck – but this does need to be made from fresh chestnuts, not canned chestnut purée. You will need patience when peeling chestnuts, so enlist some help.

SERVES 4–6

- 115g (4oz) butter
- 115g (4oz) onions, thinly sliced
- 450g (1lb) fresh chestnuts
- salt and freshly ground black pepper

Melt 55g (2oz) butter in a saucepan, add the onions and cook gently until golden brown, stirring occasionally. Meanwhile, peel the chestnuts by plunging them into a bowl of boiling water for about 10 minutes or until the shells are softened enough for you to prick a sharp knife through them. Drain the chestnuts and, with a sharp knife, loosen the skin and peel them.

Coarsely chop the chestnuts and add them to the onions with the remaining butter and salt and pepper. Cook very gently for about 20 minutes, or until the chestnuts are softened, stirring occasionally. Use the stuffing to stuff your chosen bird.

Below: Wine in gravies is not traditional but a welcome adoption as far as I'm concerned

RED WINE AND BERRY JAM GRAVY

Most gravies are best made as described in the recipes for roasts, by using the juices of the meat. Sometimes, though, you need to make a gravy from scratch and this is often the case with vegetarian roasts. This is a fruity, rich gravy which my family loves. You can use any jam, but blackberry and blackcurrant are my favourites.

SERVES 4–6

- 2 teaspoons plain flour
- 2 teaspoons butter
- 1 tablespoon berry or currant jam (or jam of your choice)
- 2 teaspoons soya sauce
- 1 dessertspoon tomato ketchup
- 175ml (6fl oz) vegetable stock (or vegetable bouillon powder dissolved in boiling water)
- 175ml (6fl oz) red wine

Start off with a *beurre manie*, or more prosaically, the flour finger-kneaded into the butter! Place this in a shallow pan and stir in the jam, soya sauce, tomato ketchup, stock and red wine.

Heat, stirring until thickened and hot, adding more liquid if necessary. You can then serve this as it is, or stir it into the meat juices in the roasting pan before serving.

MINT AND REDCURRANT JELLY

The use of redcurrant jelly can jazz up the traditional mint sauce, but don't serve it if you are also serving Red Wine and Berry Jam Gravy (see above) – only use it with a plain gravy. The

obvious partner for this is roast lamb, but it is also delicious with roast chicken, ham and cold cuts of meat.

SERVES 4–6

- 85g (3oz) redcurrant jelly
- 2 teaspoons finely grated orange zest (make sure the orange is not waxed – if it's organic, it won't be)
- 2 teaspoons chopped fresh mint

Stir all the ingredients together until well mixed, then serve.

CRANBERRY AND ORANGE PRESERVE

By soaking half the cranberries in the wine, the texture of this preserve is made more interesting, as some of the cranberries are soft and plump while the unsoaked ones have a lovely chewy texture.

SERVES 4–6

- 225g (8oz) dried cranberries
- 175ml (6fl oz) red wine
- 1 orange
- 115g (4oz) sugar
- orange juice, to thin the sauce (optional)

Place 115g (4oz) cranberries in a bowl, add the wine, stir to mix and leave to soak for about 1 hour. Finely grate the zest of the orange, then peel and segment the orange, discarding any pips. Place the soaked cranberries and wine, the remaining dried cranberries, the orange zest and orange segments in a blender or food processor and blend until coarsely chopped.

Spoon the mixture into a saucepan and stir in the sugar. Bring to the boil, then reduce the heat and simmer for about 30 minutes, or until the mixture is soft and sticky, stirring occasionally. Serve.

This makes quite a rough-textured preserve; if you prefer a smoother texture, cool the preserve slightly, then return it to the blender or food processor and blend with a little orange juice until you achieve the desired consistency. Once cooled, this will keep in a covered container in the refrigerator for about 2 weeks.

Sweetened sauces and preserves have long been used to accompany meat
Top: Mint and Redcurrant Jelly
Above: Cranberry and Orange Preserve

GINGER AND CASHEW NUT SAUCE

SERVES 4

Place 225g (8oz) plain toasted cashew nuts (toast them by roasting on a baking tray in the top of a preheated oven at 220°C/425°F/Gas Mark 7 for 5 minutes), 350ml (12fl oz) water, 1 teaspoon grated peeled fresh root ginger and 1 tablespoon soya sauce in a blender or food processor and blend until well mixed, adding more water if the mixture is too thick. You can blend this sauce to the texture you like – either slightly crunchy or smooth. Pour the mixture into a saucepan and heat gently until hot, stirring. Serve.

MUSTARD SAUCE

SERVES 4–6

300ml (½ pint) double cream
1 tablespoon mustard (any type)
1 teaspoon lemon juice
salt, to taste

Gently heat the cream in a saucepan and simmer until it thickens and reduces by about one-third. Remove the pan from the heat, whisk in the mustard first, then the lemon juice and salt to taste. Serve.

BREAD SAUCE

Serve with poultry, turkey or game – a wonderful British dish.

SERVES 4–6

1 small onion
4 cloves
300ml (½ pint) milk

6 black peppercorns
1 bay leaf
85g (3oz) fresh breadcrumbs
25g (1oz) butter
1 teaspoon freshly grated nutmeg
4 tablespoons double cream
salt and freshly ground black pepper

Stud the onion with the cloves. Pour the milk into a small saucepan and add the onion, peppercorns and bay leaf. Bring slowly to the boil, then remove the pan from the heat and set aside to infuse for about 30 minutes.

Remove and discard the onion and strain the milk into a clean pan. Bring the milk to the boil, stir in the breadcrumbs, then return to the boil and simmer for about 5 minutes, stirring. Stir in the butter, nutmeg and cream and season to taste with salt and pepper. Serve.

APPLE AND CINNAMON SAUCE

Serve this with pork or duck – I like to combine a sour cooking apple with a sweet eating apple.

SERVES 4-6

225g (8oz) cooking apples such as Bramley
225g (8oz) eating apples such as Cox's Orange Pippin
25g (1oz) sugar
1 cinnamon stick

Peel and core the cooking and eating apples and slice them thinly. Place them in a heavy-based saucepan and sprinkle with the sugar and 2 tablespoons water. Place the cinnamon stick on top.

Cover and cook gently for about 15 minutes, stirring occasionally. Remove the pan from the heat, then remove and discard the cinnamon stick. Beat the apples with a fork until they are fluffy. Serve.

HORSERADISH AND CRÈME FRAÎCHE SAUCE

This sauce is wonderful with smoked salmon, trout, roast beef and cold cuts of meat. If you grate your own horseradish, stand well back – the fumes will irritate your eyes and get up your nose.

SERVES 4–6

If using fresh horseradish, mix 2 tablespoons freshly grated horseradish with 2 teaspoons sugar and 2 teaspoons lemon juice. Mix this with 150ml (¼ pint) crème fraîche and serve.

Alternatively, mix 4 tablespoons ready-made horseradish sauce with 150ml (¼ pint) crème fraîche and serve.

Above: Traditional Bread Sauce – enriched with double cream
Opposite: We sell this Mustard Sauce in our shops with our oven-roasted sausages

summer feasts

My first two recipe choices for this section are both from the French region of Provence – and both involve liberal use of garlic!

But they suit English summers perfectly, too, and I can think of no better choice for Sunday lunch in the garden or open air than these delicious dishes. And we still feel we're feasting in the open air when it rains and we have to take shelter in the greenhouse!

AÏOLI PLATTER

Aïoli is a strong garlic mayonnaise, often referred to as the 'butter of Provence', and it is used as a dip for all manner of things which are eaten with your hands. You can have a purely vegetarian platter, or add cooked fish and meats such as mutton.

At its most simple, as described by Elizabeth David, the platter could be ham accompanied by potatoes and vegetables in season with the aïoli in a bowl at the centre of the dish, but at its grandest, *le grand aïoli* will comprise a variety of cooked meats, fish and vegetables.

The vegetables are cooked one by one in boiling stock, and the fish is then poached in the same water. Any chicken or mutton should be boiled before adding the vegetables. Choose a colourful combination of vegetables and arrange them on the largest platter you can find, or assemble on individual dishes if serving as a starter.

SERVES 6

6 globe artichokes
lemon juice
salt and freshly ground black pepper
225g (8oz) green beans
225g (8oz) carrots, sliced lengthways
225g (8oz) broccoli florets
450g (1lb) firm white fish fillet such as haddock (or you can use salmon fillet)
about 300–425ml (½–¾ pint) vegetable stock
600ml (1 pint) Mayonnaise (see recipe on page 81)
10 fat cloves garlic, crushed
12 new potatoes, cooked in their skins and cooled
225g (8oz) small tomatoes, quartered
2 red peppers, deseeded and sliced lengthways into strips
6 hardboiled eggs, shelled and cut in half
6 pieces cooked chicken or ham or a mixture (each piece about 85g/3oz in weight) – boiled mutton is also delicious for this dish

With organic artichokes, it is a good idea to soak them in a bowl of cold water with a little lemon juice added for about 30 minutes, to remove the insects.

Drain the soaked artichokes and prepare them by cutting off the stem close to the base and trimming the top of the leaves with a sharp knife. Snip off the tops of the lower leaves and pull away and discard any loose leaves from the base with your fingers. Remove and discard the hairy 'choke', by pulling it away from the heart with your fingers. This sounds terribly complicated, but you will pick it up in no time.

Place the prepared artichoke heads in a pan of lightly salted, boiling water, cover and simmer for about 30–40 minutes or until the leaves pull out easily. Drain upside down in a colander, while you prepare the other vegetables.

It is important not to overcook the vegetables. They should still be crunchy and fresh, so you really only need to blanch them. To do this, blanch the beans, then the carrots, then the broccoli florets, one after the other, by immersing them in a saucepan of boiling water for a minute or so before fishing them out and refreshing in cold water. Drain well and set aside.

Opposite: Fill a hollowed-out artichoke with creamy Aïoli as a centrepiece for this dish

Place the fish and seasoning in a shallow pan, pour over enough stock to cover the fish, adding extra stock if necessary. Cover and gently poach the fish for about 5–10 minutes, or until it is cooked but still firm. Drain well and cut the fish into bite-sized pieces. Set aside.

Make the aïoli. Mix the mayonnaise and garlic together – it is even better if you can add the garlic while making the mayonnaise. This sauce is supposed to be stiff with garlic, but of course you can reduce this if you don't like it too strongly flavoured. Set aside.

Assemble the dish. Place the artichokes in the centre of a large platter or plates. Fill each artichoke with some aïoli for dipping. Arrange all the cooked and raw vegetables, eggs, chicken or ham and fish around the artichokes. Serve.

PROVENÇAL FISH STEW

You really can ring the changes with fish stews. Use what you can find, keeping a good balance of whatever firm fish is available, and if you can't get enough fresh seafood it is fine to use frozen.

SERVES 6

50ml (2fl oz) olive oil, plus extra for brushing
2 onions, finely chopped
1 leek, washed and roughly chopped
2 tomatoes, skinned, deseeded and chopped
2 cloves garlic, crushed
1 or 2 sprigs of fresh herb fennel or a pinch of dried fennel
2 bay leaves
salt and freshly ground black pepper
300ml (½ pint) dry or medium white wine
2 tablespoons tomato purée
1.2 litres (2 pints) fresh mussels in their shells, de-bearded and scrubbed
24 large fresh clams in their shells
1½ teaspoons saffron threads
1kg (2¼lb) mixed skinless white fish fillets such as bass, snapper, red mullet, halibut and John Dory, cut into bite-sized pieces
24 large fresh prawns or crayfish, shelled and de-veined
225g (8oz) squid, cleaned and cut into rings
1.2–1.4 litres (2–2½ pints) fish stock
1 French stick or baguette, thickly sliced
4 tablespoons aïoli (optional; see recipe on page 126)
1 tablespoon chopped fresh parsley

Heat the 50ml (2fl oz) oil in a large saucepan, add the onions and leek and sauté gently for about 25 minutes or until transparent and lightly coloured, stirring occasionally. Add the tomatoes, garlic, fennel, bay leaves and salt and pepper and shake the pan over the heat for a few minutes to extract the flavours.

Pour in the wine, then bring to the boil and skim. Stir in the tomato purée, then add the mussels, clams and saffron. Cover and simmer for 5 minutes, then add the fish pieces, prawns and squid. Ladle in sufficient stock to cover the fish, adding extra stock if necessary, then cover with a tight-fitting lid and cook gently for about 5–10 minutes, or until the fish is cooked but still firm.

Meanwhile, preheat the oven to 150°C/300°F/Gas Mark 2. Lay the bread slices on a baking sheet, brush with oil, then bake in the oven for about 5 minutes, or until crisp. Spoon a thick layer of the aïoli, if using, on top of the toasted bread.

Remove and discard the fresh fennel and bay leaves from the stew, then taste and adjust the seasoning. Ladle the fish stew into bowls and serve with the aïoli-topped toast alongside. Sprinkle with chopped parsley and serve.

PAELLA

My most memorable food experiences were in France and Spain, during the years when I lived in these countries. And few have been more memorable than the classic paella dishes I tasted in the restaurants and beach bars of Valencia and Andalucia.

Opposite: You can vary this Provençal Fish Stew with whatever fish you have

A paella can be simple or elaborate and have a variety of ingredients – the only constants found in all paellas are rice, saffron and olive oil. Spaniards prefer to cook their paellas in the open air, and all along the Spanish holiday costas you can see vast paelleras being shaken and stirred over roaring fires. The flavour of wood smoke is an important ingredient in itself. But, if you cannot cook over an open fire or charcoal grill, then the best option is in the bottom of your oven.

SERVES 6

12 chicken pieces such as legs, thighs or breasts (about 700–900g/1lb 9oz–2lb total weight)
salt and freshly ground black pepper
6 tablespoons olive oil
225g (8oz) squid, cleaned and cut into rings
55g (2oz) lean boneless pork, cut into 5mm (¼in) cubes
1 onion, chopped
4 cloves garlic, finely chopped or crushed
1 red or green pepper, deseeded and cut into strips about 4cm (1½in) long and 5mm (¼in) wide
1 large tomato, skinned, deseeded and finely chopped
550g (1¼lb) long-grain or short-grain rice (if you want to be a purist, go to a Spanish delicatessen and ask for paella rice, but you can use any type)
¼ teaspoon saffron threads, crushed with the back of a spoon
1.4 litres (2½ pints) boiling vegetable stock
6 or more large raw prawns, de-veined and shelled but with heads and tails left on for effect
6 fresh clams in their shells, scrubbed
6 fresh mussels in their shells, de-bearded and scrubbed
85g (3oz) fresh or frozen (thoroughly defrosted) peas
2 lemons, each cut lengthways into 6 wedges

Season the chicken pieces all over with 1 teaspoon salt and some freshly ground black pepper. Heat 3 tablespoons oil in a large, heavy-based frying pan until a light haze forms above it, then add the chicken, skin side down, and fry until well browned, turning frequently. When the chicken pieces are a rich golden brown colour, remove from the pan, place on a plate and set aside.

Add the squid to the pan and sauté for about 1 minute, then remove from the pan, place on a plate and set aside. Discard the fat left in the frying pan. Add the remaining oil to the pan and heat until hot. Add the pork and cook quickly, until browned all over, stirring frequently. Add the onion, garlic, pepper strips and tomato and mix well. Cook quickly, stirring continuously, until most of the liquid has evaporated. This mixture is called a *sofrito* and is the basis for many Spanish dishes.

Preheat the oven to 200°C/400°F/Gas Mark 6 (or if using a charcoal grill, allow about 1 hour for the coals to burn down). Place the *sofrito*, rice, saffron and salt to taste in a 35cm (14in) paella dish (or ovenproof frying pan or casserole dish about 35cm/14in diameter and 5–6cm/2–2½in deep). Pour in the boiling stock and, stirring continuously, bring to the boil over a high heat.

Remove the pan from the heat immediately and taste and adjust the seasoning. Arrange the chicken, squid, prawns, clams and mussels on top of the rice mixture and scatter the peas at random over the top.

Set the pan on the floor of the oven and bake, uncovered, for about 25–30 minutes or until all the liquid has been absorbed by the rice and the rice grains are tender but not too soft. At no point should the paella be stirred after it has been put in the oven.

To cook on a charcoal grill, place the pan on top of the grill and cook gently for about 30 minutes, shaking the pan occasionally. Test the rice from time to time as you near the end of the cooking time to make sure that you don't overcook it.

Remove the pan from the oven or grill, cover with a clean tea towel and allow the paella to rest for about 5 minutes. Garnish with the lemon wedges, take it to the table and serve.

Opposite: Evoke the flavours of Spain with this colourful Paella

grilling and barbecues

When I lived in Spain, we ran an open-air barbeque restaurant on the hillside overlooking the sea. In the summer, people were drawn from miles around by the savoury smells of marinated and roasted meat and vegetables.

Char grilling was, of course the human's first effort at cooking, but the modern-day cook should take care not to over-char the meat. Charcoal-fired grills have been blamed for adding to Los Angeles' notorious smogs, so barbecues are not quite the idyllic mode of cooking we imagine and it is wise to limit your consumption of char-grilled meat in the interests of health, too. Barbecued foods are, however, delicious and fun – you may like to know that a water pistol is a good way to damp down any unexpected flames!

For indoor grilling, you get the best results with a grill pan with a ridged base, though of course you can pan-grill on any heavy pan. Always brush grills and pans with a little olive oil before you start and don't forget that grilling needs constant attention.

To my mind marinating is an underestimated way of cooking, as it does not take long to brew a marinade and it is a good way to preserve meat a little longer in the fridge. It will have a tenderizing effect on meats that are to

Above: Thread chunks of onion, mushroom, pepper and tomato as well as meat onto your skewers to bump up the family's vegetable consumption

be grilled or barbecued, as well as producing delicious juices for gravies. You can, of course, marinate food which is to be pan-fried or oven-roasted with equal success.

RED WINE MARINADE

Use this as a marinade for beef steaks, allowing about 225g (8oz) beef per person. I marinate the beef in this mixture overnight.

SERVES 4–6

2 tablespoons olive oil
1 onion, sliced into thin rings
4 cloves garlic, finely chopped or thinly sliced
1 tablespoon fennel seeds
1 tablespoon dried basil
2 teaspoons dried marjoram
225g (8oz) skinned tomatoes, chopped
225ml (8fl oz) red wine
125ml (4fl oz) balsamic vinegar
1 teaspoon salt
freshly ground black pepper, to taste
1 tablespoon chopped fresh parsley, to garnish

Heat the oil in a heavy-based saucepan, then add the onion and garlic and sauté for about 15 minutes, or until softened, stirring occasionally. Do not overcook: the onions should still be crunchy. Add the fennel seeds, basil and marjoram and cook for a further 5 minutes, stirring occasionally.

Add the tomatoes, wine and vinegar to the pan and season to taste with the salt and pepper. Simmer for a further 15 minutes, stirring occasionally.

Right: Beef steaks in Red Wine Marinade

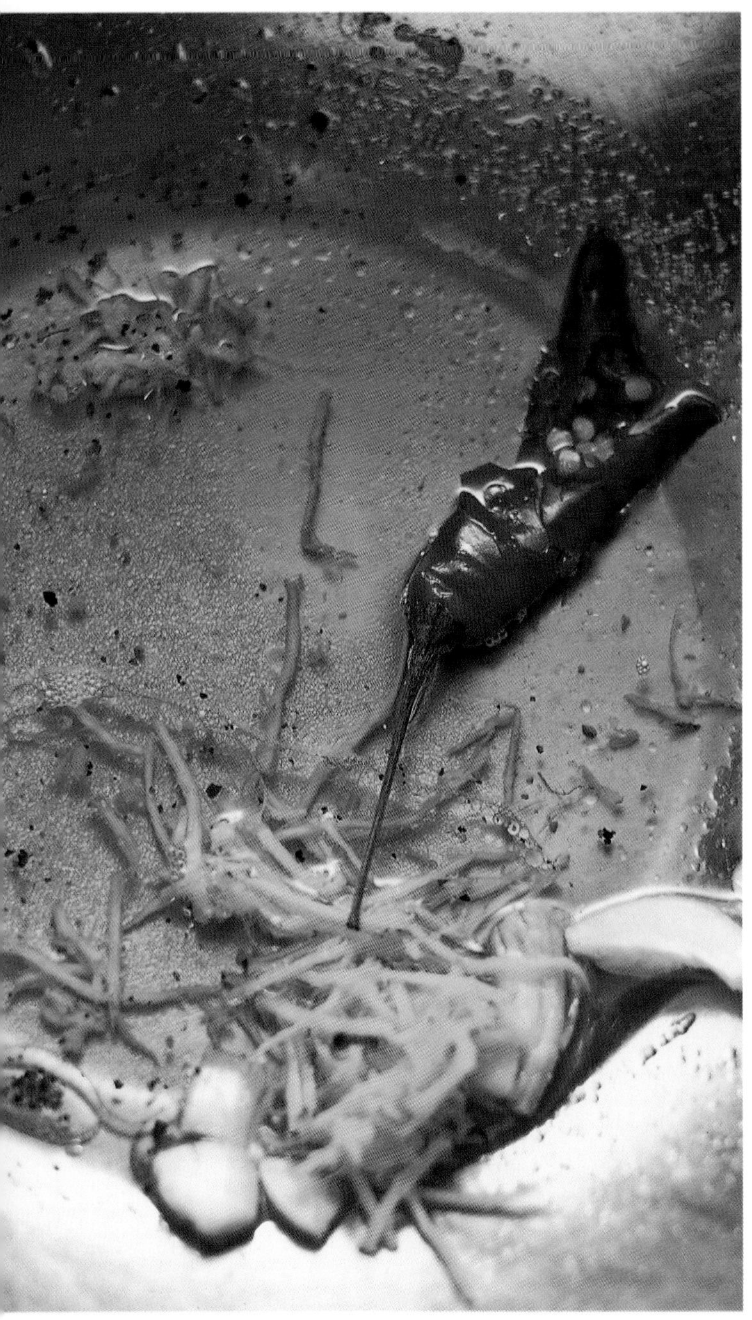

Above: The longer the Hot Ginger and Chilli Marinade stands the hotter it is!

Remove the pan from the heat and set aside to cool. Once cool, use as required to marinate meat or vegetables in the refrigerator for at least 2 hours, but preferably overnight, before grilling or barbecuing. Garnish the cooked meat or vegetables with the chopped parsley.

HOT GINGER AND CHILLI MARINADE

Use this as a marinade for beef or tofu kebabs (allow about 225g/8oz meat or tofu per person).

SERVES 4–6

- 3 tablespoons dry sherry or sake
- 1 tablespoon soya sauce
- 1 tablespoon sesame oil
- 1cm (½in) piece fresh root ginger, peeled and grated
- 1 fresh chilli, deseeded and finely chopped, or 1 dried chilli, crushed
- 1 clove garlic, crushed
- 1 teaspoon sugar
- salt and freshly ground black pepper

Place all the marinade ingredients in a small bowl and whisk together until thoroughly mixed. Use as required. If using to marinate meat or tofu, cut the meat or tofu into bite-sized pieces, place in a dish and pour over this marinade. Stir until coated all over, leave to marinate in the refrigerator for at least 2 hours, then drain, reserving the marinade.

Thread the meat or tofu onto skewers and barbecue over hot coals for about 6 minutes, or until cooked, turning and basting with the marinade occasionally.

SWEET AND SOUR MARINADE

Use this recipe as a marinade for spare ribs or vegetable skewers. Allow about 450g (1lb) spare ribs per person.

SERVES 4–6

6 tablespoons pineapple juice
4 tablespoons cider or white wine vinegar
3 tablespoons soya sauce
3 tablespoons olive oil
140g (5oz) sugar
1 teaspoon peeled grated fresh root ginger or ¼ teaspoon ground ginger

Place all the ingredients in a bowl with 6 tablespoons water and mix together thoroughly. Use as required.

If using to marinate ribs or vegetable skewers, pour this marinade over the ribs or vegetable skewers, turning to coat them all over. Leave to marinate in the refrigerator for at least 2 hours, but preferably overnight.

Grill or barbecue the ribs or skewers, brushing them with the marinade occasionally during cooking.

Left and below: Marinades are a great way to add different flavours – fruity, hot or spicy or sweet and sour – before grilling, pan-frying or roasting

CITRUS MARINADE

Use this mix as a marinade for chicken pieces. Allow about 225g (8oz) chicken per person.

SERVES 4–6

3 tablespoons olive oil
1 onion, finely chopped
2 cloves garlic, crushed
125ml (4floz) dry or medium white wine
4 tablespoons sugar
2 tablespoons tomato purée
2 tablespoons Worcestershire sauce
finely grated zest and juice of 1 orange
juice of 2 lemons
salt and freshly ground black pepper

Heat the oil in a saucepan, add the onion and garlic and sauté until soft and golden, stirring occasionally. Add all the remaining ingredients and mix well, then cover and simmer for 20 minutes, stirring occasionally. Taste and adjust the seasoning, then set aside to cool.

Strain the mixture, discard the contents of the sieve, then pour the cooled marinade over the chicken pieces. Turn the chicken pieces in the marinade to coat them all over and leave to marinate in the refrigerator for at least 2 hours.

Grill or barbecue the chicken, brushing the chicken with the marinade occasionally during cooking.

FRUIT SKEWERS

If you are barbequing, it is lovely to have a fruit dish to finish up with. Why not try these fruit skewers bathed in lemon and honey – just the thing for a balmy summer evening.

MAKES 12 SKEWERS

2 oranges, peeled with the pith removed
1 small fresh pineapple, peeled and cored
1 eating apple, peeled and cored
2 ripe mangoes or papaya, peeled and stoned or deseeded
3 kiwi fruit, peeled
½ cucumber
115g (4oz) runny honey
juice of 1 lemon

Cut all the fruit and the cucumber into big chunks, place on a plate and chill in the refrigerator until ready to cook and serve.

Just before serving, preheat the grill to medium. Thread the mixed fruit and cucumber onto 12 bamboo skewers.

Mix the honey and lemon juice together and brush all over the skewered fruit. Grill for about 5 minutes or until lightly browned all over, turning occasionally. Serve hot with any remaining honey and lemon sauce.

picnicking

I have to confess that most of my picnicking has been done at the races!

With a brother who trains horses, I am often invited to a race meeting with an offhand 'Oh, and bring something for us to eat, will you?' Picnics like that are usually eaten out of the boot of the car under an umbrella.

We also have a family tradition of going to the open-air theatre every year, which gives us the opportunity for a really slap-up picnic. On those occasions we take tiny smoked salmon sandwiches, oozing with butter and laced with lemon juice and black pepper. This is accompanied by our favourite vintage organic champagne to start the feast. We then continue with any (or all!) of the following.

OVEN-BAKED SESAME CHICKEN

The American favourite Chicken Maryland was the model for the popular breadcrumbed chicken nuggets or joints which are now served in various guises in the Kentucky Fried Chicken chain and Macdonald's – so make enough to satisfy the demand! This is a healthier version, too, as oven-baking takes the place of frying and the breadcrumb coating is glued on with yoghurt.

SERVES 4

1.3kg (3lb) oven-ready chicken or 12 smallish joints of skinless chicken such as thighs, drumsticks or breast halves
450ml (16fl oz) Greek yoghurt
salt and freshly ground black pepper
280g (10oz) dried breadcrumbs to roll the chicken in (if you only have fresh bread, make this into breadcrumbs in the food processor and then dry out in a preheated oven at 150°C/300°F/Gas Mark 2 for about 15 minutes)
55g (2oz) sesame seeds

If you are using a whole chicken, remove the skin, then divide the chicken into small joints. Mix the yoghurt with the seasoning in a bowl, then dip each chicken joint into the yoghurt, making sure it is thoroughly coated.

Mix the breadcrumbs and sesame seeds together, then dip the yoghurt-coated chicken into the breadcrumb mixture. Pat the breadcrumbs firmly onto the chicken to coat all over, then leave to dry for about 15 minutes.

Meanwhile, preheat the oven to 180°C/350°F/Gas Mark 4. Grease a baking tray and place the chicken pieces on it. Bake in the oven for 45–60 minutes, or until the chicken joints are cooked and browned (prick the chicken with a fork in the thickest parts – if the juices run clear, the chicken is cooked). Serve hot or cold. If you are eating this at home, it is traditional to serve it with fried bananas and Corn Fritters (see recipe on page 26).

SPICY PICKLED PRAWNS

Although you need to leave this dish for a minimum of 24 hours, you can keep the prawns for two or three days. Use the big, sweet Mediterranean prawns that are now widely available. I have allowed 4 prawns per person, but why not have more? My Mediterranean family say that as well as the tails we should keep the heads on, as they like to pull them off and suck them!

SERVES 4

16 large raw Mediterranean prawns or king or tiger prawns
1 red onion, thinly sliced
1 small red pepper, deseeded and sliced
1 small yellow pepper, deseeded and sliced
175ml (6fl oz) olive oil
50ml (2fl oz) cider vinegar
juice of 2 lemons
1½ teaspoons Worcestershire sauce
1½ teaspoons tabasco sauce
1 teaspoon mustard powder or 2 teaspoons Dijon mustard
1 teaspoon sugar
½ teaspoon salt
1 tablespoon chopped fresh coriander

Take the shells and heads off the prawns, but leave the tails on as they are more attractive this way. De-vein the prawns by cutting a slit along the back of each with a small, sharp knife and lifting out and discarding the black thread with the point of the knife. Place the prawns in a bowl with the onion and peppers and set aside.

Place all the remaining ingredients in a bowl and whisk together until thoroughly mixed. Pour over the prawn mixture, toss to mix, then cover and refrigerate for at least 24 hours, stirring once or twice.

Place the prawn mixture and marinade in a saucepan, bring to the boil, then reduce the heat and simmer for 3–5 minutes, or until the prawns are cooked. Remove the pan from the heat and allow the prawns to cool in the liquid. Serve or chill before serving.

STUFFED VINE LEAVES

Stuffed vine leaves are an excellent picnic food as the leaves serve as a wrap for the contents, turning the whole package into perfect finger food.

MAKES 24

24 preserved medium vine leaves
1 tablespoon olive oil
1 bunch spring onions, finely chopped
1 clove garlic, crushed
115g (4oz) long grain white rice
115g (4oz) pine nuts
115g (4oz) sultanas
115g (4oz) canned (drained) chopped tomatoes or fresh tomatoes, chopped
115g (4oz) ricotta cheese
1 tablespoon chopped fresh mint
salt and freshly ground black pepper
juice of 1 lemon

Drain the vine leaves, separate them and rinse under running water. Drain and set aside. Heat the oil in a frying pan, add the spring onions and sauté until softened, stirring occasionally. Add the garlic and rice and stir to mix, then add all the remaining ingredients, except the lemon juice, and mix well. Remove the pan from the heat.

Lay a vine leaf vein-side up with the stem towards you. Place about 1 tablespoon of the filling at the base of the leaf and roll up, tucking in the excess leaf at the sides to make a small bundle. Repeat with the remaining vine leaves and filling.

Place the bundles upright in a saucepan and squeeze the lemon juice over them. Add enough cold water to cover the bundles, then weigh them down by placing 1 or 2 small plates on top. Bring to the boil, then reduce the heat, cover and simmer for about 1 hour, or until the rice is cooked. Serve with Greek yoghurt seasoned with salt and lemon juice.

SPANISH TORTILLA

This tastes particularly good when it is cold and so makes the perfect picnic food. Take it in the pan it was cooked in, with the wedge-portions already marked out. If you are making a driftwood fire, you could even heat the wedges up.

To a basic potato omelette, I add ham and chopped fresh parsley. Omit the ham if you are vegetarian or make 2 tortillas, one with ham and the other without – they will certainly be eaten!

SERVES 4

- 3 medium potatoes, cut in half
- salt and freshly ground black pepper
- 2 tablespoons olive oil
- 1 large onion, finely chopped
- 6 eggs
- 115g (4oz) cooked ham, roughly chopped
- 1 tablespoon finely chopped fresh parsley
- 25g (1oz) butter

Cook the potatoes in a saucepan of lightly salted, boiling water for about 10 minutes, or until just tender – do not overcook. Drain and cool, then cut into small dice.

Heat 1 tablespoon oil in a non-stick frying pan (if you are not using a non-stick pan, heat some salt on the base of the frying pan before using and then wipe it off – this will prevent the eggs from sticking). Add the onion and fry gently until just softening, stirring occasionally. Add the potatoes and fry until both the onion and potatoes are browning, stirring occasionally.

Remove the pan from the heat. Whisk the eggs in a bowl with a seasoning of salt and pepper to taste, then stir in the onion and potato mixture, the ham and the parsley.

Wipe the frying pan clean, then add the remaining oil and the butter to the pan. Heat until the butter is melted and the fat is hot, then pour in the egg mixture and shake the pan once or twice.

Reduce the heat and leave the omelette to cook slowly until the underside is browned and the mixture is set but still moist. Loosen the sides of the omelette with a palette knife and place a plate the size of the pan over the pan.

This is where the fun begins and everybody loves to try! Turn the frying pan over onto the plate so that the omelette slips onto it, then place the pan back on the hob and slide the omelette back into the pan to cook the second side. Cook again until the omelette is browned underneath. Cut into wedges and serve hot or cold.

Opposite: I regard this Tortilla as a 'lusty omelette'. The Spanish and Italians (who call it frittata) view it as a staple in their diet

family favourites

Most family members have a favourite meal – food they would like served on their birthday, for instance. I asked my family to devise their favourite formal meal, and this is what they came up with. I have given a starter and main dish for each menu; you can select a dessert of your choice from Chapter 6.

MY HUSBAND'S MENU

Bryn likes little bits of things to start – antipasti or hors-d'oeuvres such as butter beans with tuna, finely chopped cooked beetroot or olives with garlic and herbs. He particularly likes this next recipe, followed by a traditionally raised organic gammon joint.

ONIONS À LA GRECQUE

SERVES 4

450g (1lb) small pickling onions
2½ tablespoons olive oil
1½ teaspoons runny honey
90ml (3fl oz) dry white wine
1 teaspoon tomato purée
salt and freshly ground black pepper
55g (2oz) raisins
1 tablespoon finely chopped fresh coriander

Bring a saucepan of water to the boil, then blanch the onions still in their skins in the boiling water for 1 minute. Tip into a colander, then rinse under cold running water and drain. Remove the skins carefully using a small sharp knife.

Place the peeled onions in a heavy-based saucepan with the oil, honey, wine, tomato purée, seasoning and 150ml (¼ pint) water and stir to mix. Bring to the boil, then reduce the heat, cover and simmer for about 25 minutes or until the onions are tender, shaking the pan from time to time and making sure the onions don't catch.

Add the raisins to the pan and cook, uncovered, for a further 5–10 minutes, or until most of the liquid has been absorbed, stirring occasionally. Taste and adjust the seasoning and stir in the coriander. Serve warm or cold.

ROAST HONEY-GLAZED GAMMON WITH CUMBERLAND SAUCE

It is extremely difficult to gauge the saltiness of cured gammon joints, as modern methods of curing are far less salty than they used to be. If you are buying organic and traditionally cured meat, the following recipe will be fine; otherwise, check with your supplier or read the instructions on pre-packed joints.

SERVES 8–10

1.8kg (4lb) lean boneless gammon joint
1 onion, peeled and cut in half
2 bay leaves
12 peppercorns
2 tablespoons wholegrain mustard
2 tablespoons runny honey
12 cloves

Place the gammon joint in a large pan with the onion, bay leaves and peppercorns. Add enough water to cover well, then bring to the boil and skim off any scum that forms. Cover and simmer for 2 hours.

Preheat the oven to 220°C/425°F/Gas Mark 7. Strain the gammon and cut off the rind – do this by cutting two horizontal lines along the top and peeling back the long strips. Score the fat into squares or with criss-cross cuts to make a diamond pattern if liked.

Mix the mustard and honey together and smear the mixture all over the meat and fat. Stud the fat with the cloves and place in a baking tin. Bake in the oven, uncovered, for 30 minutes or until the gammon is a glazed golden colour.

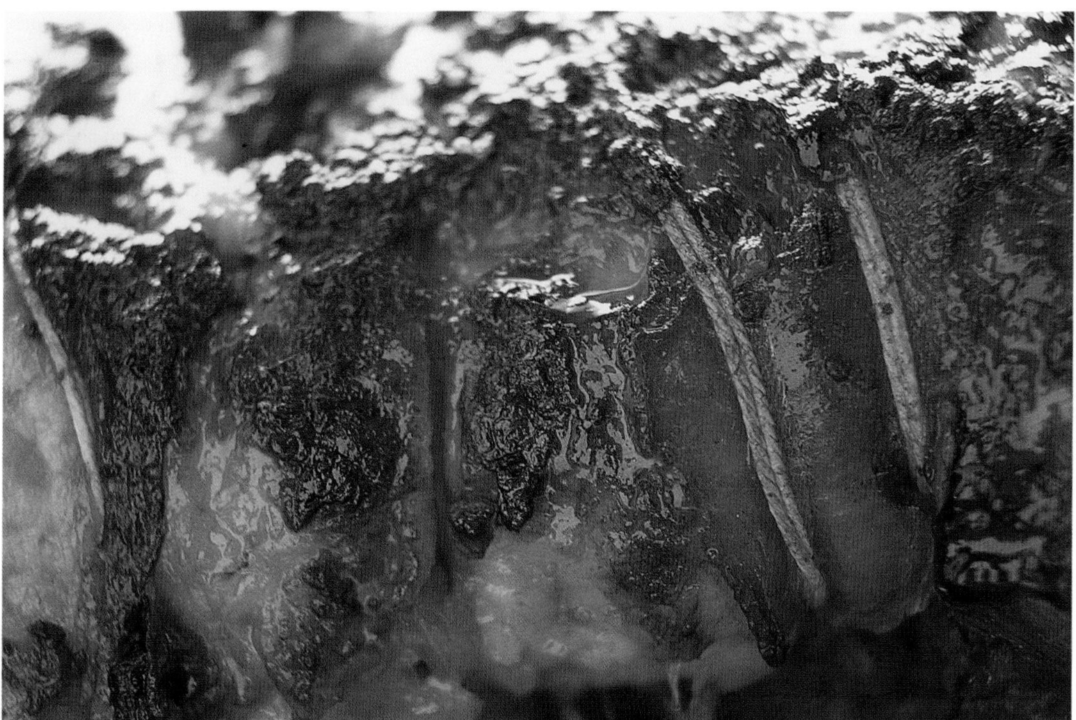

Above: Succulent, lean gammon encrusted with a honey and mustard glaze

If you are serving the gammon hot, leave it to rest for about 30 minutes before carving and serving. Otherwise, set aside to cool, then chill before carving and serving. Serve with Cumberland Sauce (see recipe below), boiled new potatoes smothered in butter and chopped fresh parsley, and garden peas.

CUMBERLAND SAUCE

This version has a little chilli added to it to give it an extra zing, but it is optional – so if in doubt, leave it out!

SERVES 8–10

2 oranges
1 lemon
6 tablespoons redcurrant jelly (make sure the jelly has a high currant content)
6 tablespoons port
1 teaspoon mustard powder
1 teaspoon ground ginger
½ teaspoon chilli powder
2 tablespoons red wine vinegar
salt and freshly ground black pepper

Thinly pare the zest from the oranges and lemon using a potato peeler and cut the zest into thin strips. Place these strips in a saucepan, add 300ml (½ pint) water and bring to the boil. Boil for 5 minutes, then strain and set aside. Squeeze the juice from the oranges and lemon and set aside.

Place the redcurrant jelly and port in a saucepan and heat gently until the jelly has melted, stirring. Mix the mustard powder, ginger and chilli powder with the vinegar until smooth and blended, then add this to the pan and stir to mix. Bring to the boil and simmer for 5 minutes, stirring occasionally.

Add the fruit juices, return to the boil and simmer for a further 5–10 minutes, or until the mixture is syrupy, stirring occasionally. Add seasoning to taste, mix in the reserved strips of pared zest and pour into a serving bowl. Set aside to cool and always serve cold.

MY DAUGHTER'S MENU

My daughter Harriet is half Spanish and she spent most of her childhood holidays in southern Spain, where seafood is a way of life. Prawns of all shapes and sizes are her 'big thing' – hence her choice of starter.

PRAWN COCKTAIL

The one stipulation Harriet makes is that this recipe is made with a mixture of prawns. You can use both frozen and fresh.

SERVES 6

72 small prawns (about 12 per person), frozen (cooked) and thawed or cooked and shelled
18–24 king prawns (about 3–4 per person), raw or cooked
12 tiger prawns (about 2 per person), raw or cooked
7 tablespoons Mayonnaise (see recipe on page 81)
4 tablespoons Tomato Ketchup (see recipe on page 15)
3 tablespoons double cream
2 teaspoons lemon juice
1½ teaspoons brandy
salt and freshly ground black pepper
1 small lettuce, shredded
1–2 tablespoons vinaigrette
1 lemon, cut into 6 wedges
1 tablespoon finely chopped fresh parsley

If you need to cook the prawns, place them in a saucepan, cover with water and poach them for 2–5 minutes, depending on their size, until cooked. Remove the pan from the heat and allow the prawns to cool in the cooking liquid.

Drain, then peel the prawns, if necessary. I always leave the tails on large prawns as they look a little odd without. If you are using frozen cooked prawns, thaw them completely and drain well. Set aside.

Make the sauce. Place the mayonnaise, tomato ketchup, cream, lemon juice, brandy and seasoning in a bowl and mix well. Add the small prawns and toss to mix. Set aside.

Place the shredded lettuce in the base of 6 glass or china dishes. Drizzle over a little vinaigrette and toss the lettuce with your fingers or a fork. Place the small prawns and sauce on top of the dressed lettuce.

Garnish with the king prawns and lemon wedges. Sprinkle the parsley over the top and chill in the refrigerator for at least 30 minutes before serving. If you want to be swanky, omit the lettuce and serve the prawns and cocktail sauce in double glass bowls, where the top bowl is set over crushed ice in the bowl underneath.

SHANGHAI DUCK

This recipe is delicious served hot or cold. Double up the recipe if you like, as it will always get eaten.

SERVES 4

8 leeks
2.25kg (5lb) oven-ready duck with giblets
125ml (4fl oz) dry sherry
125ml (4fl oz) soya sauce
1 tablespoon runny honey
1cm (½in) piece fresh root ginger, peeled and grated, or ½ teaspoon ground ginger
3 carrots, cut lengthways into thinnish strips

Prepare the leeks by trimming off the roots and discarding the tough outer leaves. Cut off the white part of the leeks about 15cm (6in) from the root end, wash

Opposite: Use a mixture of prawns for a new take on this traditional Prawn Cocktail

thoroughly, drain, cut into strips, then set aside. Wash the remaining green part of the leeks, then slice them and place them in the bottom of a large heavy-based saucepan, which is big enough to take the duck.

Remove the giblets from the duck and trim away any fatty pieces of skin from the duck. Rinse and dry the duck, then place it breast side down on top of the leeks with the giblets tucked down the side.

Mix the sherry, soya sauce, honey, ginger and 175ml (6fl oz) water together, then pour into the pan over the duck and bring to the boil. Reduce the heat, cover and simmer for 30 minutes. Turn the duck over, so that it is breast side up, and baste it with the cooking liquid. Cover and simmer for a further 1 hour, basting the duck occasionally with the cooking juices.

Skim off the fat from the surface of the cooking liquid and remove and discard the giblets. Arrange the white leeks and carrots around the duck and return to the boil. Cover and simmer for a further 20 minutes or until the duck and vegetables are cooked, basting occasionally and adding a little more water if the sauce is becoming too dry. Skim off any fat from the sauce.

Place the cooked duck on a board and carve the meat, peeling back and discarding the soft skin as you go. Serve immediately on cooked plain rice or noodles, with the vegetables and sauce spooned over.

MY SON'S MENU

Nick's choices reflect his peripatetic life. He lived from the ages of 7 to15 in southern Spain and later travelled extensively in Latin America.

SCALLOP CEVICHE FROM PERU

This marinated raw seafood dish is eaten with great gusto on the seafront in Peru, washed down with cocktails made from the local hooch, egg white and lime juice, shaken together with crushed ice.

SERVES 4

450g (1lb) raw shelled scallops
1 small fresh red chilli, deseeded and finely chopped
1 small red pepper, deseeded and cut into small strips
2 shallots, finely chopped
1 tomato, deseeded and chopped
1 clove garlic, crushed
225ml (8fl oz) fresh lime juice
1 tablespoon lemon juice
1 teaspoon sugar
1 tablespoon finely chopped fresh coriander
2 tablespoons finely chopped fresh parsley, plus extra to garnish
salt and freshly ground black pepper
1 avocado, peeled, stoned and cut into 8 slices

Place all the ingredients, except the avocado, in a large glass bowl. Gently toss the ingredients together to mix, making sure the scallops are well coated with the juices. Cover and refrigerate for at least 5 hours or until the scallops lose their translucent appearance, stirring occasionally.

Garnish with the avocado slices and extra chopped parsley and serve.

POLLO FROM MARBELLA

SERVES 4

1.1kg (2½lb) oven-ready chicken, cut into 8 pieces
2 cloves garlic, crushed
1 tablespoon red wine vinegar
1 tablespoon olive oil
1½ teaspoons dried oregano
4 ready-to-eat pitted dried prunes, cut in half if large
8 pitted green olives
1½ teaspoons capers (not drained)
2 bay leaves
½ teaspoon salt

Opposite: Pollo from Marbella recalls the flavours of southern Spain

½ teaspoon freshly ground black pepper
55g (2oz) sugar
175ml (6fl oz) dry white wine
1 tablespoon finely chopped fresh parsley

Place the chicken pieces in a large bowl with the garlic, vinegar, oil, oregano, prunes, olives, capers and their juice, bay leaves and salt and pepper, and stir to mix well. Cover and leave to marinate in the refrigerator overnight.

When you are ready to cook the chicken, preheat the oven to 180°C/350°F/Gas Mark 4. Arrange the chicken pieces in a single layer in a shallow ovenproof dish. Spoon the marinade over the chicken pieces and sprinkle them with the sugar. Pour the wine around the chicken.

Bake in the oven for about 1 hour, or until the chicken pieces are cooked and tender, basting them frequently with the marinade. Check that the chicken is cooked by piercing the thickest parts of the joints with a fork – when the juice runs clear and not bloody, the chicken is cooked. Remove and discard the bay leaves. Transfer the chicken, prunes, olives and capers to a warmed serving plate and sprinkle with the chopped parsley. Pour the juices from the dish into a jug and pass round separately.

Nick's choice of vegetables to accompany his feast are mashed potatoes, followed by a green salad tossed in balsamic vinaigrette (see recipe on page 80).

MY DAUGHTER-IN-LAW'S MENU

Kate is a vegetarian and complains about having a raw deal in our largely carnivorous company, although we eat a lot less meat than before and are enjoying adapting our family meals to offer her a better selection.

Opposite: Vegetarian Shish-kebab basted with Red Wine Marinade and served on a bed of rice

BRAISED LEEKS WITH BUTTERED PARMESAN CRUMB TOPPING

Coming from Tom Jones' country, it's no surprise that my daughter-in-law likes leeks, the national emblem of Wales.

SERVES 6

6 leeks
1.2 litres (2 pints) well-seasoned vegetable stock
175g (6oz) butter
115g (4oz) fresh breadcrumbs
55g (2oz) parmesan cheese, grated

Prepare the leeks. Wash them thoroughly in running water – be careful, as organic vegetables come with the dirt still on. Trim and discard the roots and the tough outer leaves, then cut each leek in half from top to bottom and rinse well again under running water.

Bring the stock to the boil in a saucepan, add the leeks, cover and simmer for about 15 minutes or until tender. Drain well, then lay the leeks in a shallow serving dish and keep hot. Preheat the grill to high.

Meanwhile, melt the butter in a shallow pan, add the breadcrumbs and cook until golden all over, stirring continuously. Stir in the parmesan, then spoon the breadcrumb mixture evenly over the leeks. Brown under the grill, then serve with a fresh tomato salsa.

VEGETARIAN SHISH-KEBAB

Prepare a Red Wine Marinade and assemble the kebabs on long wooden skewers. This recipe provides for 2 skewers per person. The kebabs can be oven-roasted, pan-grilled or barbecued – whichever method you use, remember to baste them frequently with the marinade during cooking.

SERVES 6

1 quantity Red Wine Marinade (see recipe on page 133)
24 large button mushrooms

1 small aubergine, cut into 4cm (1½in) chunks
2 onions, cut into 2.5cm (1in) chunks
1 red pepper, deseeded and cut into chunks
1 yellow or green pepper, deseeded and cut into chunks
6 tomatoes, cut into quarters

Place the marinade in a large bowl, add the mushrooms, toss to mix and set aside. Cook the aubergine chunks in a saucepan of boiling water for about 10 minutes, or until tender but firm. Drain well, then add them to the marinade while still hot. Set aside and leave to marinate at room temperature for at least 3 hours.

Preheat the oven to 190°C/375°F/Gas Mark 5, or preheat the grill to high, or if using a charcoal grill, allow about 1 hour for the coals to burn down. To assemble the kebabs, remove the mushrooms and aubergines from the marinade using a slotted spoon and place on a plate. Reserve the marinade. Thread all the vegetables alternately onto 12 wooden skewers, until all the ingredients are used up.

Place the vegetable kebabs on a rack in a baking tin, on a grill or barbecue rack or on an oiled griddle pan and brush them all over with the marinade.

Cook the vegetable kebabs in the oven, under the grill, over hot barbecue coals or over a medium heat on the hob, until cooked, lightly browned and *al dente*, basting frequently with the marinade during cooking. Serve the kebabs on a bed of cooked rice, with any juices from the pan poured over.

MY OWN FAVOURITE

RICOTTA AND PARMESAN TART

I like to serve this tart with slow-roasted oven-dried tomatoes on the side.

SERVES 4–6

25g (1oz) butter
175g (6oz) fresh parmesan cheese, finely grated
350g (12oz) ricotta cheese
2 tablespoons chopped fresh basil
1 tablespoon chopped fresh flat-leaf parsley
125ml (4fl oz) double cream
2 eggs, beaten
salt and freshly ground black pepper

Preheat the oven to 190°C/375°F/Gas Mark 5. Mix the butter with 55g (2oz) parmesan and use this to grease the inside of a 20cm (8in) springform cake tin. Set aside.

Place the ricotta, herbs and cream in a bowl and stir until well mixed. Gradually add the eggs, mixing well. Fold in the remaining parmesan, then season to taste with salt and pepper.

Spoon the mixture into the prepared tin and level the surface. Bake in the oven for about 20 minutes or until lightly set and a golden crust has formed over the top surface. Serve immediately in slices.

BEEF STROGANOFF

Perhaps it's my age and misty-eyed nostalgia for those first trendy bistros which London sported in the Sixties, when eating out with wine became accessible to more people. Stroganoff was often the most sophisticated and expensive dish on the menu in those days and I still love it!

SERVES 4–6

3 tablespoons butter
3 tablespoons olive oil

- 2 onions, sliced
- 450g (1lb) mushrooms, thinly sliced
- 900g (2lb) beef fillet, cut into thin slices
- 2 tablespoons tomato purée
- 2 tablespoons Worcestershire sauce
- 1 tablespoon Dijon mustard
- 1 tablespoon paprika
- 225ml (8fl oz) double cream
- 225ml (8fl oz) soured cream
- salt and freshly ground black pepper
- 2 tablespoons finely chopped fresh parsley

Place half the butter and half the oil in a heavy-based frying pan and heat until the butter has melted. Add the onions and sauté until soft and browning, stirring occasionally. Transfer the onions to a bowl and set aside. Add the mushrooms to the pan and sauté them until soft, stirring occasionally. Add the mushrooms to the onions in the bowl. Add the remaining butter and oil to the pan and heat until the butter has melted. Add the slices of beef to the pan in batches and sauté over a high heat until just lightly browned, turning once. Remove the meat from the pan as it is cooked and place it on a plate. Set aside.

Mix the tomato purée, Worcestershire sauce, mustard, paprika and 1 tablespoon water together. Add this mixture to the pan and heat gently while you stir the mixture, scraping the juices and sediment which have been left by the meat from the bottom of the pan. Add the onions and mushrooms to the pan, then mix the two creams together and add this to the pan with the seasoning. Simmer for about 5 minutes, stirring occasionally. Add the meat, then simmer for a further 2 minutes or until the meat is heated through, stirring occasionally. Serve immediately, garnished with the parsley.

FEEDING A CROWD

We all have times when we need to entertain a crowd, whether it's on Bonfire Night or for a teenage disco. Serve with a selection of salads and lots of garlic bread.

CHILLI CON CARNE

SERVES 20

- 4 tablespoons olive oil
- 800g (1¾lb) onions, chopped
- 2 green peppers, deseeded and chopped
- 2.7–3.6kg (6–8lb) lean minced beef (for vegetarians, replace the mince with soya protein)
- 1½ tablespoons freshly ground black pepper
- 1½ tablespoons tomato purée
- 3 tablespoons crushed garlic
- 85g (3oz) ground cumin
- 115g (4oz) chilli powder
- 115g (4oz) Dijon mustard
- 4 tablespoons salt
- 4 tablespoons dried oregano
- four 400g (14oz) cans chopped tomatoes, drained
- 225ml (8fl oz) red wine
- 125ml (4fl oz) lemon juice
- four 400g (14oz) cans red kidney beans, rinsed and drained
- 4 tablespoons finely chopped fresh parsley
- a little beef or vegetable stock

Heat the oil in a large pan, add the onions and peppers, cover and cook gently for about 10 minutes or until softened, stirring occasionally. Add the minced beef and cook over a medium heat until the meat is browned all over, stirring occasionally.

Reduce the heat and stir in the black pepper, tomato purée, garlic, cumin, chilli powder, mustard, salt and oregano. Add the tomatoes, wine and lemon juice and mix well. Bring to the boil, then reduce the heat, cover and simmer for 45 minutes, stirring occasionally.

Add the kidney beans and parsley and mix well. Stir in a little stock if the mixture looks a bit dry. Bring to the boil, then simmer, uncovered, for 15 minutes, or until the meat is cooked, stirring occasionally. Serve with cooked rice or flat noodles, bowls of sour cream and garlic bread.

celebration dinner

This celebration dinner is for times when we really want to push the boat out, such as Christmas Eve or Thanksgiving.

Serve mini blinis with caviar or organically farmed smoked salmon and hand them round while you sip champagne – organic, of course. Follow the Blinis recipe on page 28 and use the best caviar you can afford. These days, you can even get a vegetarian caviar. For dessert, I would choose Fruit and Ricotta Cheese Pie (see recipe on page 162).

OYSTERS IN CHAMPAGNE SAUCE

As a 17-year old, I found myself in the heart of gastro-Bourgogne-land, living with a wealthy bourgeois family. Sunday lunch always started with oysters and champagne, even though Maman frugally patched and darned the sheets!

Many people don't get on with oysters, which is a shame as they are very high in proteins and minerals – especially zinc, which makes us more fertile! But they can be treacherous to open and you will need to use an oyster knife. If you get help at this stage, it can be fun – don't do it alone in case you stab yourself.

To open, wrap your left hand (or right if you're left-handed) in a tea towel, then place the oyster cup-side down with the hinge towards you and insert the knife into the hinge, pushing and twisting simultaneously. You will need to cut the muscle under the top shell by sliding the knife along the length of it. Be careful that you don't lose the juices in the process.

It is wise to eat oysters in season – which is the winter months (the months with an 'r' in them). Ideally,if you can get them, oysters should be the native, wild kind.

For this glamorous celebration starter, I suggest you serve 4 oysters per person.

SERVES 8

- 55g (2oz) butter
- 1 small onion, finely chopped
- 1 bay leaf
- 175ml (6fl oz) champagne (or cava or sparkling wine)
- 150ml (¼ pint) fish stock
- 300ml (½ pint) double cream
- juice of ½ lemon
- salt and freshly ground black pepper
- 32 fresh oysters

Melt the butter in a saucepan, add the onion and bay leaf and cook for 1–2 minutes, or until the onion is softened but not coloured, stirring occasionally. Add the champagne, bring to the boil, then reduce the heat and simmer until the mixture is reduced in volume by two-thirds.

Pour in the fish stock, return to the boil, then simmer until reduced by two-thirds once again. Stir in the cream and cook gently for a further 6 minutes or until the sauce starts to thicken slightly, stirring occasionally.

Remove and discard the bay leaf, then stir in the lemon juice and season to taste with salt and pepper. Pour into a bowl and whisk with a hand whisk or hand blender until smooth. Serve with the oysters.

ROAST SADDLE OF LAMB

Saddle of lamb is without doubt my favourite meat. It is succulent and tender, and very good to look at when it comes to the table.

SERVES 8

1 saddle of lamb, weighing about 2.7–3.6kg (6–8lb)
55g (2oz) butter
salt and freshly ground black pepper
350ml (12fl oz) dry white wine
425ml (¾ pint) lamb or vegetable stock
1 tablespoon plain flour

Preheat the oven to 200°C/400°F/Gas Mark 6. Weigh the lamb and calculate the cooking time, allowing 15–20 minutes per 450g (1lb), plus 15–20 minutes. Spread the butter all over the saddle of lamb and season with black pepper. Place in a roasting tin and pour the wine and 150ml (¼ pint) of the stock over the joint.

Roast in the oven for the calculated cooking time, basting every 15 minutes. Add a little extra stock if the liquid reduces too much. Test the meat with a sharp knife until it is cooked to your liking, then transfer to a plate and keep warm while you make the gravy.

Tip or spoon the fat carefully from the juices, leaving all the sediment behind in the tin. Add the flour to this, mixing fast with a wooden spoon. Cook slowly on the hob until coloured, stirring, then pour in the remaining 300ml (½ pint) stock. Still stirring, bring to the boil then reduce the heat and simmer until the gravy is well reduced. Season to taste with salt and pepper, then strain and pour into a gravy boat.

To carve, run the knife around and under the meat, then cut across the meat almost down to the bone and place on a warm dish. You can then take the whole saddle to the table and serve it easily. Serve with cauliflower in a nutmeg-flavoured white sauce, Pommes Boulangère, Ratatouille, Carrots Glazed with Honey and Nutmeg, and Mint and Redcurrant Jelly (see pages 91, 118 and 122).

fruit desserts, drinks and ices

Fresh fruit is the most valuable food in the world. Each individual fruit is a little nugget of nutrition, rich in vitamins – there is no richer source of the all-important vitamin C than those purple blackcurrants, blackberries, blueberries and cranberries – as well as minerals, fibre and natural sugars to fuel our brains and bodies. So make fruit the heart of your family's diet and encourage everyone to eat several pieces each day.

Most people enjoy fresh fruit just as it comes. But making fresh fruit salad, jellies, fruit ices or lollies, ice creams, fruit tarts, cakes, fruit salsas and coulis is fun for all the family and encourages people to eat more of it, while freshly squeezed juice gives a higher percentage of vitamins than shop-bought fruit juice.

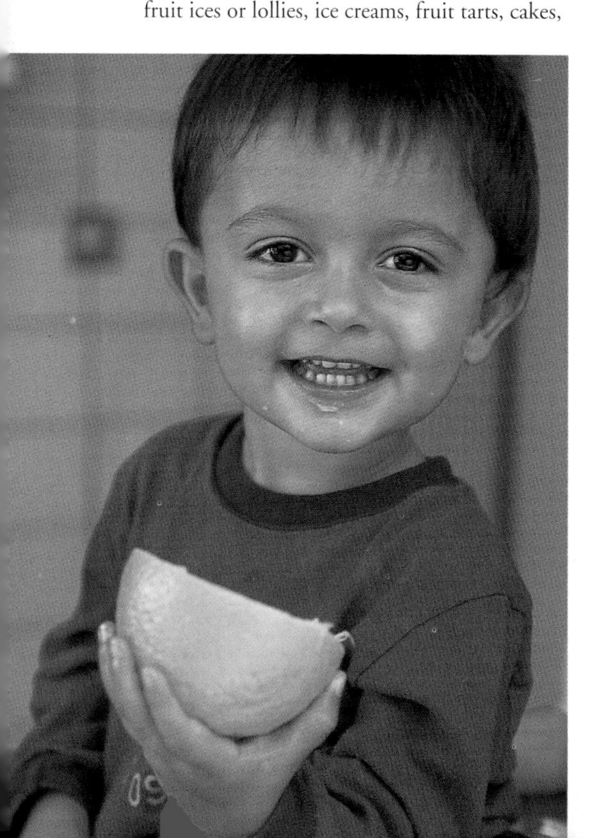

One of the things that is missing from the way we eat today is the 'hunter-gathering' or 'grower-gathering' element which ensures that the fruit comes to us straight from the branches with little or no loss of vitamins. Most fruit is sold on to us after being stored for many days (non-organic will probably have been sprayed with chemicals to keep it from rotting). This is why – unless you can ensure a fast delivery from the farm, as with vegetable box schemes – eating organic fruit frozen soon after harvesting is often better than choosing so-called fresh fruit which has been lurking on greengrocers' or supermarket shelves for a few weeks.

Yet we still have access to wild and cultivated fruit that we can gather straight from the plant. Many gardens have elder bushes, for instance, which give two possible crops – the flower and the berry. Both can be used to make cordial or jelly and, of course, wine! Blackberries can still be found in profusion in the hedgerows and crab apple trees also grow wild. And why not take an organic picnic into the country and see what you can find?

Make fruit the only pudding in your household and you and your family will be well on the way to healthy eating.

compôtes and jellies

Fresh organic fruit is harder to find in the winter, so we use a lot of dried organic fruit – which is just as rich in vitamins and minerals as the fresh variety. If you're really stuck, you can use juice (organic, of course) as well. Add fresh fruit or berries if you have them.

The discovery of BSE in cattle became an issue not just for beef but also for many other foods that we eat, including sweets, jellies and many of other processed foods, so always check the label. Traditionally, gelatine is made from cattle bones and if you have not already done so you should change to a vegetarian gelling agent, such as Gelozone or agar agar. For more information, see page 16. Whichever gelling agent you choose, always follow the manufacturer's instructions on how to use it.

Remember that a home-made jelly does not set clear and sparkling like a bought one. It will be cloudy and dense-looking, but will taste delicious!

DRIED FRUIT COMPÔTE

This is good made with any dried fruit, either one type such as apricots or pears, or a mixture. Remember to use the organic, unsulphured ones, which have been dried in the sun.

SERVES 4–6

450g (1lb) of any or all mixed dried fruit of your choice, such as raisins and sultanas and chopped ready-to-eat apricots, apples, pears, peaches, prunes and dates
125ml (4fl oz) maple syrup
a pinch of salt

Place the fruit, maple syrup and 125ml (4fl oz) or more water in a heavy-based saucepan. Bring gently to the boil, then simmer, uncovered, on a very low heat for about 15–30 minutes or until the fruit is soft, stirring occasionally. Add more water if it becomes too thick, then stir in a pinch of salt to bring out the flavours. Remove the pan from the heat and set aside to cool. This is delicious eaten on its own or puréed and folded into Greek yoghurt.

FRUIT JUICE COMPÔTE

This is a wonderful pudding base for fresh fruit and you can use either yoghurt or cream to fold in with the fruit. A topping of chopped nuts turns it into a fancy pudding.

SERVES 4–6

850ml (1½ pints) fresh or bottled fruit juice (a mixture of juices will make it more exotic)
125ml (4fl oz) maple syrup or 90ml (3fl oz) runny honey
juice of ½ lemon
½ teaspoon ground cinnamon
½ teaspoon ground nutmeg
4 tablespoons cornflour or Kuzu (see page 16)
300ml (½ pint) Greek yoghurt or whipped double cream
115g (4oz) prepared fresh fruit, such as coarsely grated apples and chopped strawberries

Reserve 125ml (4fl oz) fruit juice and set aside. Place the remaining fruit juice in a saucepan with the maple syrup or honey, lemon juice and ground spices and bring to the boil, then reduce the heat.

Blend the cornflour or, preferably, Kuzu with the reserved fruit juice. Stir the mixture into the hot fruit juice, then cook gently for about 5 minutes, or until the mixture is thick and smooth, stirring from time to time. Pour into a large bowl and whisk until light and fluffy with an electric beater or wire whisk (if you are using a hand whisk this will take about 15 minutes!). Set aside to cool. Fold in the yoghurt or whipped cream until well mixed, then serve topped with the fresh fruit.

Opposite: Vary the consistency of this Dried Fruit Compôte to make a sauce by adding more liquid and blending when cooked – delicious with vanilla ice cream.

ORANGE JELLY

SERVES 4

175g (6oz) sugar
6g (⅛oz) gelling agent
3 oranges, washed
1 lemon, washed

Measure 300ml (½ pint) water in a jug, then set aside 4 tablespoons of this water in a cup. Pour the remaining water into a saucepan and add the sugar. Heat gently until the sugar has dissolved, stirring, then bring the mixture to the boil and boil for about 20 minutes, to make a sugar syrup. Sprinkle the gelling agent over the reserved water. Remove the pan from the heat and add the gelling agent mixture to the syrup, stirring until dissolved. Set aside.

Using a potato peeler, finely pare the zest from the oranges and lemon and place in a bowl. Pour the hot syrup over the fruit zest. Squeeze the juices from all the fruit and add to the mixture in the bowl, stirring well. If necessary, add some extra orange juice to the mixture to make the volume up to 600ml (1 pint).

Set aside for 1 hour, so that all the flavour is extracted from the fruit zest, then strain into a jug. Pour the mixture into a wetted 600ml (1 pint) mould or bowl and chill in the refrigerator until firm and set. Turn out onto a plate and serve with home-made ice cream, crème fraîche or cream.

MANGO JELLY

SERVES 4

175g (6oz) sugar
600ml (1 pint) unsweetened mango juice
6g (⅛oz) gelling agent
1 mango, peeled, stoned and sliced

Place the sugar in a heavy-based saucepan and heat gently until it has dissolved and you have a clear golden sugar syrup, stirring occasionally. Remove the pan from the heat.

Reserve 3 tablespoons mango juice in a cup and set aside. Add 150ml (¼ pint) of the remaining mango juice to the pan and return to a low heat, cooking until the sugar syrup and mango juice blend together, stirring frequently. Sprinkle the gelling agent over the reserved 3 tablespoons mango juice and set aside. Add the remaining mango juice to the pan and bring to the boil, stirring. Add the gelling agent mixture to the pan and stir until dissolved. Remove the pan from the heat and set aside to cool.

Place the mango slices in the bottom of small serving bowls or dishes and pour some mango jelly mixture over the top, dividing it equally between them. Cover and leave to set overnight in the refrigerator. Serve with whipped cream.

Opposite: Home-made jellies are cloudy and more chewy than the shop-bought version

pastryless pies

Most people don't have time to make pastry and find it a bit daunting even when they do. They would rather buy the ready-made version.

At the time of going to press, no organic equivalent to ready-made pastry is available (although I am sure it will come), so I have given recipes which do not use pastry cases and are therefore quick and easy to make.

BANANA SOUR CREAM PIE

I like this pie because it has an unusual combination of ingredients and is not too sweet.

SERVES 6–8

- 225g (8oz) digestive biscuits, crushed
- 55g (2oz) mixed nuts, finely chopped
- ½ teaspoon ground cinnamon
- ½ teaspoon grated nutmeg
- 115g (4oz) butter, melted
- 350g (12oz) cream cheese
- 125ml (4fl oz) sour cream
- 55g (2oz) runny honey
- 2 tablespoons fresh lemon juice
- 1 large ripe banana, peeled and mashed
- 1 teaspoon vanilla extract
- ¼ teaspoon almond extract

Preheat the oven to 180°C/350°F/Gas Mark 4. Grease a deep 23cm (9in) pie dish and set aside. Place the biscuit crumbs, nuts and ground spices in a bowl and stir to mix. Add the melted butter and mix well, then press the mixture firmly and evenly over the base and sides of the prepared dish.

Bake in the oven for 10 minutes, then remove from the oven and set aside to cool. Refrigerate the biscuit base while you prepare the filling.

To make the filling, place all the remaining ingredients in a bowl and beat together until smooth and well mixed. Pour into the chilled biscuit crust and level the surface. Chill for a further 3 hours or until set. Cut into squares or slices and lift out with a spatula and spoon to serve.

PUMPKIN PIE

Bake this pumpkin pie in a buttered dish and serve with ice cream, cream or crème fraîche.

SERVES 6–8

- 350g (12oz) peeled, cooked and puréed pumpkin, or canned pumpkin purée
- 175ml (6fl oz) runny honey
- 2 tablespoons black treacle or blackstrap molasses
- 3 teaspoons ground cinnamon
- 1½ teaspoons ground ginger
- ¼ teaspoon ground cloves
- 1 teaspoon salt
- 4 eggs
- 450ml (16fl oz) milk

Preheat the oven to 180°C/350°F/Gas Mark 4. Grease a 23cm (9in) ovenproof pie dish and set aside. Place all the ingredients in a large bowl and beat together until smooth and well mixed.

Pour into the prepared dish, then bake in the oven for about 40 minutes, or until set and golden brown. Serve hot or cold in slices.

Opposite: Banana Sour Cream Pie has a lightly spiced nutty base

FRUIT AND RICOTTA CHEESE PIE

This is a light dessert, perfect for a summer's day or at the end of a heavy meal, when all you want is to melt something sweet and fruity in your mouth.

SERVES 6–8

900g (2lb) ricotta cheese
4 eggs
225ml (8fl oz) milk
115g (4oz) sugar
2 teaspoons vanilla extract
finely grated zest and juice of 1 lemon
225ml (8fl oz) Greek yoghurt
115g (4oz) prepared fresh fruit or berries, either single fruit or mixed
1 tablespoon maple syrup
fresh berries, to decorate

Preheat the oven to 190°C/375°F/Gas Mark 5. Grease a 20cm (8in) round springform cake tin and set aside. Place the ricotta, eggs, milk, sugar, vanilla extract and lemon zest and juice in a blender or food processor and blend until smooth, well mixed and fluffy. Pour into the prepared tin and level the surface.

Place the springform tin in a roasting tin and pour in a little warm water around the base of the springform to create a bain-marie. Bake in the oven for about 45 minutes or until set.

Remove from the roasting tin and set aside to cool completely. Chill in the refrigerator for at least 30 minutes before topping.

Place the yoghurt in a bowl and stir in the fresh fruit or berries and maple syrup until well mixed. Remove the cheesecake from the tin and place it on a plate. Spread the fruit and yoghurt mixture evenly over the top of the cheesecake, decorate with fresh berries and serve in slices.

ice creams & parfaits

What do you really need to make ice cream? Nowadays there are all sorts of ice-cream makers, available at all prices. If your family likes ice cream I really recommend you invest in one. But it is possible to make it by hand, and you will not need a machine for parfaits.

Some of the following recipes contain raw eggs and are therefore not recommended for pregnant mums, small children or elderly people.

VANILLA ICE CREAM

SERVES 6

115g (4oz) sugar
4 egg yolks
300ml (½ pint) milk
300ml (½ pint) double cream
½ vanilla pod

Place the sugar and egg yolks in a bowl and whisk together until thick and creamy, then set aside. Place the milk and cream in a heavy-based saucepan and heat gently until hot but not boiling. Gradually whisk the hot milk and cream into the egg yolk mixture, then return to the saucepan. Add the vanilla pod.

Cook over a low heat, stirring continuously, until the mixture is the consistency of thick cream, being careful not to let the mixture boil. Remove the pan from the heat and set aside to cool.

Strain the mixture through a fine sieve, then pour into an ice-cream maker and churn until frozen.

Alternatively, strain the mixture into a shallow freezerproof container, cover and freeze for about 1½ hours, or until half frozen and mushy in consistency. Tip into a chilled bowl and whisk furiously with an electric hand whisk, or whizz in the food processor, until smooth. Return the mixture to the container, cover and freeze until firm.

You can repeat this half-freezing and mashing process again if you would like a smoother ice cream, but once will do.

Remove the ice cream from the freezer and leave at room temperature for about 15 minutes before serving, to allow the ice cream to soften a little. Serve in scoops.

Below: Sprinkle this light, tangy Fruit and Ricotta Cheese Pie with a little icing sugar before serving

SUMMER FRUIT ICE CREAM

This perfumed cream dessert is a must for summer. It has a fresh, fruity flavour and a beautiful rich colour, and there is no need to stir while freezing. Make this ice cream with tart ripe berries, such as blackcurrants, redcurrants or blackberries.

SERVES 6

450g (1lb) fresh or frozen (defrosted) fruit of your choice (see above)
225g (8oz) icing sugar, sifted
juice of ½ lemon
300ml (½ pint) double cream

Rinse the fruit, then using a fork, strip the berries from the stems. Crush the fruit in a nylon sieve placed over a basin, using the back of a wooden spoon. Discard the contents of the sieve. Add the icing sugar and lemon juice to the fruit pulp/juice and stir until smooth and well mixed.

In a separate bowl, whip the cream until thick, then fold it into the fruit mixture, until well mixed. Pour the mixture into 1 or 2 shallow freezerproof containers. Cover and freeze for several hours until firm.

Remove the ice cream from the freezer and leave at room temperature for about 15 minutes before serving, to allow the ice cream to soften a little. Serve in scoops.

DAIRY-FREE ICE CREAM

A growing number of people do not get on with dairy products and, of course, the number of vegans is on the increase, too. This is a healthy dairy-free ice-cream option for everyone and is quick and easy to make.

SERVES 6

- 115g (4oz) finely ground nuts, either single nut or mixed
- 2 medium bananas, peeled and sliced
- 150ml (¼ pint) soya milk
- 1 tablespoon runny honey
- ½ small pineapple, peeled, cored and sliced, or 1 ripe mango, peeled, stoned and sliced

Place all the ingredients in a blender or food processor and blend until smooth and well mixed. Turn the mixture into a shallow freezerproof container and freeze until firm – it should be ready in about 2 hours.

Remove the ice cream from the freezer and leave at room temperature for about 15 minutes before serving, to allow the ice cream to soften a little. Serve in scoops.

FROZEN FRUIT YOGHURT

For yoghurt ice, you will certainly need an ice-cream maker otherwise you will not achieve a good texture – yoghurt does not freeze well because it is low in fat and tends to freeze into little crystals. The addition of a little gelling agent (we use the vegetarian alternative, see page 16) helps to keep the mixture smooth.

SERVES 4–6

- 55g (2oz) prepared fresh fruit, frozen fruit (defrosted) or ready-to-eat dried fruit, cut into small pieces
- 1 tablespoon jam (match the flavour to the chosen fruit)
- 600ml (1 pint) natural yoghurt (made from milk or soya milk)
- 115g (4oz) sugar
- 6g (⅙oz) gelling agent

Place the fresh or frozen (defrosted) fruit – such as peaches and apricots – in a saucepan and add just enough water to cover. Simmer for 5–10 minutes, or until the fruit is tender. If using soft fruits such as raspberries or strawberries, they will not need cooking, so simply mash them with a fork and set aside. If using dried fruits, place them in a saucepan with just enough water to cover. Simmer for about 15 minutes, or until the fruit is tender. Remove the pan from the heat and set aside until the fruit is warm.

Remove the fruit from the juices in the pan using a slotted spoon. Reserve the juices and place the fruit in a bowl. Add the jam to the warm fruit and stir to mix, then fold in the yoghurt, mixing well. Set aside until lukewarm.

Meanwhile, add the sugar to the juices in the pan and heat gently, stirring, until the sugar has dissolved. Remove the pan from the heat and set aside to cool until it is lukewarm, then sprinkle with the gelling agent. Return to the hob and heat gently until the mixture becomes clear and runny, stirring.

Alternatively, if using soft fruits such as raspberries or strawberries, dissolve the sugar in 5 tablespoons water by heating gently in a saucepan, allow the mixture to cool until it is lukewarm, then add the gelling agent and dissolve as above. Add the gelling agent syrup to the lukewarm yoghurt mixture and stir to mix well. With soft fruits, add the gelling agent syrup, jam and yoghurt to the mashed fruit and mix well. Pour into an ice-cream maker or sorbetière and churn until frozen. Serve in scoops.

BASIC FRUIT PARFAIT

You do not need an ice-cream maker to make parfaits, just a loaf tin. Try this recipe with any puréed fruit or berries, cooked or raw. If you choose a soft fruit such as raspberries, you do not need to cook them, but if you are using rhubarb it will need to be stewed before puréeing with a little sugar.

Opposite: Raspberries are a rich source of vitamin C, and unbeatable for flavour

SERVES 6

175g (6oz) sugar
3 egg whites
450g (1lb) fresh, frozen (defrosted) or canned fruit, puréed
sifted icing sugar, to taste
300ml (½ pint) double cream

Line a 900g (2lb) loaf tin with greaseproof paper and set aside. Place the sugar in a heavy-based saucepan with 300ml (½ pint) water. Heat gently until the sugar has dissolved, stirring, then bring to the boil and boil for about 5 minutes or until the syrup has thickened.

Whisk the egg whites until softly stiff, then slowly pour the hot syrup over the whisked egg whites, folding it in continuously until the mixture is stiff and glossy.

In a separate bowl, mix the fruit purée with enough sifted icing sugar to achieve the level of sweetness you like. In another bowl, whip the cream until it forms soft peaks. Fold the fruit purée into the egg white mixture and then fold in the cream until well mixed. Pour into the prepared tin and level the surface. Cover and freeze for about 7 hours or until firm.

Remove from the freezer about 15 minutes before serving to allow the parfait to soften a little. Turn out onto a plate and serve in slices. This will keep in the freezer for about 1 month.

sorbets & granitas

Sorbets, or sherbets – to give them their English name – are very easy to make with an ice-cream maker or sorbetière. It is an excellent way to give the family fruit, and for a lower-sugar sorbet you can replace the sugar with runny honey.

Granitas, on the other hand, don't require an ice-cream maker, as they are frozen sweetened fruit juices, milks or coffees. They are very popular in Spain, where they are known as granizados, and also in Italy – hence the name granita. The most popular flavours are lemon, coffee or cinnamon milk.

Fruit granitas can be made with runny honey instead of sugar, simply by adding 2 tablespoons runny honey to every 600ml (1 pint) fruit juice. This mixture is then poured into a shallow freezerproof container and placed in the freezer. Fork it around regularly, scraping the ice crystals from around the edges of the container and breaking them up into the rest of the mixture. The mixture looks like masses of grains of ice and should be ready to eat after about 3 hours.

Some of the following recipes contain raw eggs and are therefore not recommended for expectant mums, small children or elderly people.

COFFEE GRANIZADO

To make this, simply dissolve equal parts of sugar in equal parts of boiling water. As a rough guide, this would be 25g (1oz) sugar per person – so for 6 people, you would use 175g (6oz) sugar and 175ml (6fl oz) boiling water. Add to this a coffee cup of strong black coffee per person and the finely grated zest and juice of 1 lemon for every 6 people, and mix well.

Pour this mixture into a shallow freezerproof container, cover and freeze for about 1 hour, then fork the ice crystals from the edges of the container back into the liquid, mixing well. Cover and return to the freezer.

Repeat this forking process every 30 minutes for a further 2–3 hours. It is a good idea to involve children or other members of the family in this procedure as it can become a bit tedious! You can keep the granizado going for about 4 hours after this, by forking regularly, but it will not last in the freezer like a sherbet or ice cream, so serve it when it is ready. Serve with cream sprinkled with sifted cocoa powder.

Opposite: The whipped cream topping on this Coffee Granizado is sprinkled with cocoa powder to look like a cappucino

MANGO SORBET

Sorbets are simply a sugar syrup mixed with fruit juice and sometimes, but not always, stiffened with the white of an egg. Remember that for a mango sorbet you will need less sugar than for a lemon or lime sorbet, as the mangos are naturally sweeter.

SERVES 6

250g (9oz) sugar
pared zest and juice of 1 lemon
700g (1lb 9oz) fresh ripe mango flesh, puréed
1 egg white

Place the sugar in a heavy-based saucepan with 600ml (1 pint) water. Heat gently until the sugar has dissolved, stirring, then add the lemon zest. Bring to the boil and boil rapidly for 8–10 minutes or until the syrup feels tacky and a thread forms between your finger and thumb. Remove and discard the lemon zest.

Place the mango purée in a bowl. Pour the sugar syrup onto the mango purée, add the lemon juice and stir to mix well. Set aside to cool, then pour into an ice-cream maker, add the egg white and churn until frozen.

Alternatively, pour the mango mixture (without the egg white at this stage) into a shallow freezerproof container and freeze for 2 hours. Spoon the mixture into a chilled bowl and beat with a whisk or fork until smooth. In a separate bowl, whisk the egg white until foamy, then fold it into the mango mixture. Return this mixture to the container, cover and freeze for a further 1 hour.

Once again, spoon the mixture into a chilled bowl, then beat until smooth. Return to the container, cover and freeze again for 1 hour, then beat the mixture until smooth once again. Return to the container and freeze until firm.

Remove from the freezer and leave to stand at room temperature for 10 minutes, before serving in scoops.

LEMON SORBET

It is fun to serve this sorbet in the hollowed lemons themselves. To do this, cut off one-third of each lemon at the pointy end and grate the zest from the small piece only, then squeeze the juice from all the lemons. Remove the remaining pith to make large lemon cups and cut a thin slice from the base so that they will stand level. Chill in the fridge while you make the sorbet.

SERVES 6

450g (1lb) sugar
finely grated lemon zest (see above)
450ml (16fl oz) fresh lemon juice
1 egg white
sifted icing sugar and fresh mint sprigs, to decorate

Place the sugar in a heavy-based saucepan with 450ml (16fl oz) water. Heat gently until the sugar has dissolved, stirring, then bring to the boil. Reduce the heat and simmer for 15 minutes. Remove the pan from the heat and set aside to cool.

Stir in the lemon zest and lemon juice, mixing well, then pour into a shallow freezerproof container. Cover and freeze for 3 hours, then spoon into a chilled bowl and beat with an electric whisk or hand whisk until smooth. At this point, whisk the egg white in a separate bowl until foamy, then fold it into the lemon mixture. Return this mixture to the container, cover and freeze for a further 1 hour. Once again, spoon the mixture into a chilled bowl, then beat until smooth. Return to the container, cover and freeze again for a further 1 hour or until firm.

Remove from the freezer and leave to stand at room temperature for 10 minutes, before scooping into the chilled lemon cups. Decorate with sifted icing sugar and mint sprigs and serve.

Opposite: Dress a simple Lemon Sorbet by serving in hollowed lemons.

syllabubs

Syllabubs – or fools – are quick and delicious. Syllabubs are the dressier version, usually served at dinner parties because of the alcohol content.

Make with just cream for a sumptuous dessert or with half cream and half custard or with Greek yoghurt for a more everyday dessert or for diet-conscious people. The whipped cream version will be much lighter and fluffier. Fools are more everyday and child-friendly. Gooseberries always crop up in fool recipes, because they are easy to grow yet are not very popular eaten fresh.

GOOSEBERRY FOOL

SERVES 6

450g (1lb) gooseberries, topped and tailed, or any other berries
85g (3oz) sugar
425ml (¾ pint) double cream

Place the gooseberries or other berries in a stainless steel saucepan with the sugar and 1 tablespoon water. Cook gently until the fruit is soft and swollen, stirring occasionally. Remove the pan from the heat and either mash the fruit with a fork for a rough-textured fool, or cool slightly, then purée the fruit in a blender or food processor for a smoother fool. Set aside to cool.

Whip the cream in a bowl until it thickens but not into stiff peaks. Fold the mashed fruit or fruit purée into the cream, mixing well.

Spoon into individual glass dishes and chill in the refrigerator for at least 15 minutes before serving.

Opposite: Orange and Lemon Syllabub – so easy, so pretty and *so* delicious!

BLACKCURRANT FOOL

SERVES 6

350g (12oz) blackcurrants, stalks removed
85g (3oz) sugar
425ml (¾ pint) double cream or Greek yoghurt
fresh mint sprigs, to decorate

Wash the blackcurrants and drain them well, then place in a saucepan with the sugar and 1 tablespoon water. Cover, bring to the boil over a gentle heat, then simmer for about 5 minutes or until the fruit is tender but not mushy, stirring occasionally.

Remove the pan from the heat and cool slightly, then purée the fruit and juices in a blender or food processor until smooth. Press the purée through a nylon sieve and discard the contents of the sieve. Set the purée aside to cool.

Whip the cream in a bowl until thick, then fold into the fruit purée, mixing well. Alternatively, fold the Greek yoghurt into the fruit purée, mixing well.

Spoon into individual glass dishes and chill in the refrigerator for at least 15 minutes before serving. Decorate with fresh mint sprigs.

ORANGE AND LEMON SYLLABUB

SERVES 6

2 small oranges
1 lemon
1 tablespoon brandy
1 tablespoon sweet sherry
85g (3oz) icing sugar, sifted
425ml (¾ pint) double cream

Finely grate the zest of 1 orange and the lemon. Reserve a little of the orange zest to decorate the finished syllabub. Squeeze the juice from all the fruit. Place the fruit zests in a bowl, add the orange and lemon juices, brandy and sherry and stir to mix. Set aside to soak for 2 hours.

Strain the fruit juice mixture into a bowl and discard the fruit zest. Stir the sifted icing sugar into the fruit juice until dissolved and well mixed.

In a separate bowl, whip the cream until it forms soft peaks, then fold the cream into the fruit juice, mixing well. Spoon into glasses and chill in the refrigerator for at least 15 minutes before serving. Decorate with the reserved orange zest.

BANANA CREAM SYLLABUB

SERVES 6

4 ripe but firm bananas
3 tablespoons lemon juice
3 tablespoons sweet white wine
3 tablespoons icing sugar, sifted
425ml (¾ pint) double cream

Peel the bananas, then mash them in a bowl with the lemon juice, wine and sifted icing sugar until smooth. In a separate bowl, whip the cream until softly stiff, then fold the cream into the banana mixture until well mixed.

Spoon into individual glass dishes and chill in the refrigerator for at least 15 minutes before serving.

poached fruit

Poaching fruit in syrup brings out their flavours and they can then be kept for several days in the poaching liquid, in the refrigerator.

You can poach virtually any fruit. Apples and pears should be peeled, cored and quartered; peaches and apricots should be poached whole and peeled only after they are cool.

BASIC POACHING SYRUP

THIS RECIPE IS SUFFICIENT TO POACH 450g (1lb) FRUIT.

350g (12oz) sugar
6 whole cloves
1 vanilla pod
1 cinnamon stick
finely pared zest of 1 lemon
1–2 tablespoons red or white wine (optional)

Place all the ingredients except the wine in a large, heavy-based saucepan and add 1.2 litres (2 pints) water. Heat gently until the sugar has dissolved, stirring, then bring the mixture to the boil, reduce the heat and simmer for 10 minutes.

Using a slotted spoon, remove and discard the cloves, vanilla pod, cinnamon stick and lemon zest.

Add the fruit of your choice to the syrup and bring the mixture back to a simmer. Cook the fruit gently for about 10 minutes or – depending on the fruit – until it is tender, but not mushy.

Remove the pan from the heat, stir in the wine, if using, and set aside to let the fruit cool in the syrup. Cover and chill before serving, or keep covered in the refrigerator for up to 2–3 days.

Opposite: Hot poaching syrup runs through the rich red juice of these figs

VANILLA-POACHED FRESH FIGS

Make the syrup as above, but instead of cooking the figs in the syrup, simply place the fresh figs in a dish, then cut each fig from the top into 4 quarters and open them out. Bring the syrup to the boil, stir in the wine, if using, then strain the syrup over the figs. Cool and chill in the refrigerator for at least 15 minutes before serving.

FRESH PEACHES IN SYRUP FLAVOURED WITH ORANGE AND LEMON

In a slight variation, fresh peeled peaches are covered with the poaching liquid for this recipe.

SERVES 6

6 peaches
175g (6oz) sugar
1 orange
1 lemon

Cut the peaches in half lengthways, twist the halves against each other and pull apart – they should separate neatly. Remove and discard the stones, then blanch the peach halves in a pan of boiling water for about 30 seconds.

Remove the peaches from the water using a slotted spoon, cool slightly, then peel away and discard the skins. Arrange the peach halves in a serving dish and set aside.

Place the sugar in a heavy-based saucepan with 300ml (½ pint) water. Heat gently until the sugar has dissolved, stirring, then bring the mixture to the boil. Meanwhile, thinly pare the zest from the orange and lemon. Add the fruit zests to the boiling sugar syrup, reduce the heat and simmer for 5 minutes.

Remove the pan from the heat and add the juice of the orange and lemon. Strain the syrup over the peaches and set aside to cool. Cover and chill in the refrigerator for at least 15 minutes before serving.

baked fruit

Slow baking produces a rich syrup from the fruit which combines with the other ingredients in the baking dish. It is a good way to use less-than-perfect fruit, which the family might otherwise turn their noses up at.

SPICY BAKED APPLES

Choose large cooking apples such as Bramleys, and fill with a delicious syrupy mixture of dried fruits and spices. Do not use old dried spices as they will have lost their oomph!

SERVES 6

225g (8oz) sultanas
225ml (8fl oz) apple juice or brandy, or a mixture
1 teaspoon ground cinnamon
½ teaspoon ground allspice
½ teaspoon ground cloves
85g (3oz) sugar
6 cooking apples
butter for greasing
flaked almonds and pared lemon zest, to decorate

Place the sultanas in a bowl with the apple juice or brandy or a mixture of the two (depending on whether this is destined for adults or children!) and stir to mix. Cover and leave to soak overnight.

Preheat the oven to 170°C/325°F/Gas Mark 3. Stir the cinnamon, allspice, cloves and sugar into the sultana mixture, mixing well.

Core the apples, leaving the peel on, then score around their middles with a small sharp knife. Butter an ovenproof dish, which should be big enough to let the apples

Opposite: Baked apples can be as plain or as fancy as you like

stand in without touching each other. Place the prepared apples in the dish, then fill them with the sultana mixture. Pour about 1cm (½in) water into the dish around the bases of the apples.

Bake in the oven for about 45 minutes or until the apples are soft. Serve with the syrup that has collected in the base of the dish poured over them. Decorate with almonds and lemon zest.

BAKED PLUMS

I prefer these to stewed plums as they don't disintegrate. The slow cooking means that the sugar and lemon juice form a delicious syrup.

SERVES 6

- 700g (1lb 9oz) plums
- 175g (6oz) sugar
- juice of 1 lemon

Preheat the oven to 170°C/325°F/Gas Mark 3. Wipe the plums and place them in an ovenproof casserole dish. If preferred, the plums can be halved and stoned before placing them in the dish.

Sprinkle the plums with the sugar, then drizzle over the lemon juice and 3 tablespoons water. Cover and bake in the oven for 30–40 minutes, or until the fruit is tender but still keeping its shape. Serve warm or cold with yoghurt, cream or ice cream.

BAKED FRESH APRICOTS

Apricots are one of those fruits – like strawberries – where the taste of the organically grown version is overwhelmingly better. Organic apricots taste of sunshine.

SERVES 6

- 700g (1lb 9oz) fresh apricots, washed
- 115g (4oz) sugar
- juice of 1 lemon, strained

Preheat the oven to 150°C/300°F/Gas Mark 2. Place the whole apricots in an ovenproof dish. Add the sugar and lemon juice and stir gently to mix – you will not need any water as the juice and sugar will make a delicious syrup.

Cover and bake in the oven for 45–60 minutes, or until the fruit is tender. Serve warm or cold with cream or home-made Vanilla Ice Cream (see recipe on page 163).

BAKED BANANAS AND CRANBERRIES

This is a brilliant combination of yellow banana and red jewel-like cranberries.

SERVES 6

- 175g (6oz) sugar
- 225g (8oz) cranberries
- 6 bananas
- 25g (1oz) butter, melted
- a pinch of salt

Preheat the oven to 180°C/350°F/Gas Mark 4. Place the sugar and 150ml (¼ pint) water in a heavy-based saucepan and heat gently until the sugar has dissolved, stirring.

Wash the cranberries, removing and discarding any soft berries and stalks, and add them to the sugar syrup. Bring to the boil, then reduce the heat and simmer, uncovered, for about 10 minutes or until the berries are soft, stirring occasionally.

Peel the bananas, slice them lengthways and place them in a shallow ovenproof baking dish. Brush the bananas with melted butter and sprinkle with salt. Pour the cranberry syrup evenly over the bananas, then cover and bake in the oven for 10 minutes. Uncover and bake in the oven for a further 5 minutes or until the bananas are soft. Serve hot or warm with single cream.

drinks

Why not keep home-made lemonade, freshly squeezed juice and cordial in your fridge instead of cartons of juice, squash and coke? You can buy a great range of organic cordials, but they are fun to make too.

Fruit and vegetable juice cocktails can be vital vitamin boosters, and a couple of teaspoons of powdered vitamin C (available in all chemist shops) added to fruit or vegetable juices is the perfect pick-me-up for someone who is run down or has a cold or 'flu. Vitamin C is a well-known immune booster.

If you are going to juice, you will need to invest in a juicing machine and always follow the manufacturer's instructions. It is wise, too, to invest in a book about juices, as they can help to relieve many disorders, such as eczema and arthritis.

Smoothies are a great meal in a glass if you're in a rush and are a good way to get kids to eat fruit in a drink – they are also just plain yummy!

Lemonade was the first thing my mother taught me to make and I can distinctly remember standing at the end of our drive at the age of about 6 with my two pet rabbits tied to a chair by their leads, selling lemonade by the glass. It was a very hot summer and I must have been saving for something – I just wish I could remember what!

FRUIT COCKTAIL

SERVES 1

1 medium bunch of seedless grapes, washed
1 small eating apple, cut in half and cored
¼ lemon, washed

Right: Refreshing and free from artificial sweeteners and colourings, home-made cordials are superior to any non-organic drinks you can buy in the shops

Push the grapes through the hopper (opening) of the juicing machine, followed by the apple and lemon.Pour the juice into a glass and serve immediately to benefit fully from the newly released vitamins.

VEGGIE COCKTAIL

SERVES 1

- 1 raw beetroot with top intact, washed
- a handful of fresh parsley
- 4 carrots, scrubbed
- 2 celery sticks, washed

Push the beetroot and parsley through the hopper (opening) of the juicing machine, followed by the carrots and celery. Pour into a glass and serve immediately.

Below: Lemon zest cooling for Fresh lemonade Right: No milk is needed to make this creamy, Non-dairy Smoothie

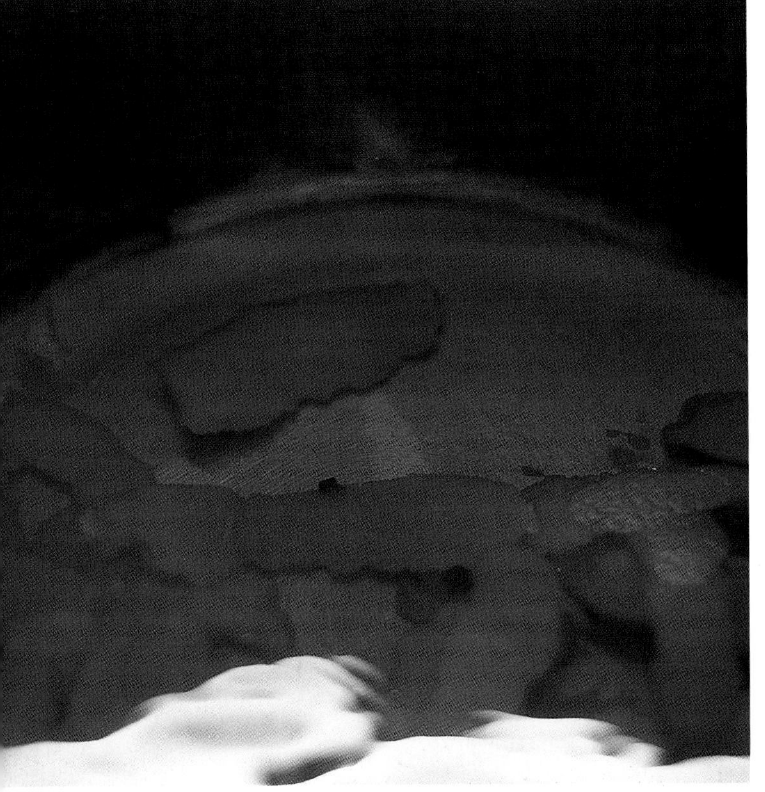

SPICY TONIC

SERVES 1

- ¼ pineapple, with its skin still on
- ½ eating apple, unpeeled, cut in half and cored
- 5mm (¼in) slice fresh root ginger, peeled

Push the pineapple through the hopper (opening) of the juicing machine, followed by the apple and ginger. Pour the juice into a glass and serve immediately.

FRESH LEMONADE

SERVES 6

- 3 lemons
- 115g (4oz) sugar

Pare the zest from the lemons and place the zest in a saucepan with 850ml (1½ pints) water and the sugar. Heat gently to dissolve the sugar, stirring, then bring to the boil and simmer for 5 minutes. Remove the pan from the heat and set aside to cool.

Squeeze the juice from the lemons and pour into a jug. Strain the cooled sugar mixture into the jug and stir to mix. Taste for sweetness and stir in a little extra sugar, if needed.

Chill in the refrigerator for at least 30 minutes before serving. Pour into glasses to serve. This lemonade will keep in the refrigerator for up to 3–4 days.

FRESH LIME JUICE

SERVES 1

- 2 limes
- 2 tablespoons sugar

Squeeze the juice from the limes and pour the juice into a jug or bowl. Add the sugar and 500ml (18fl oz) water and mix well to dissolve the sugar. Pour into a glass, adding some crushed ice if desired, and serve.

BANANA YOGHURT DRINK

Use either milk or soya milk to make this highly nutritious meal in a glass.

SERVES 1

1 banana, peeled and sliced
4 tablespoons natural yoghurt (dairy or soya)
2 tablespoons freshly squeezed orange juice
1 tablespoon milk
a grating of nutmeg

Place all the ingredients in a blender or food processor and blend until smooth, thick and well mixed. Pour into a glass and serve immediately.

NON-DAIRY SMOOTHIE

You can substitute any fruit for the berries in this smoothie and add more banana to make a thicker drink.

SERVES 1

115g (4oz) fresh or frozen (defrosted) berries
1 large banana, peeled and sliced
125ml (4fl oz) freshly squeezed orange juice

Blend all the ingredients together in a food processor or blender until the mixture is smooth and thick. Pour into a glass and serve immediately.

suppliers

Organic food is no longer hard to come by – supermarkets and wholefood shops are stocking increasingly large ranges that are growing all the time. There are other ways of buying organic products though and one of the most convenient is by mail order – I have listed companies with particular specialities below. For fruit and vegetables, local box schemes are ideal in that they put you, the buyer, directly in touch with the grower. If you can't find a local scheme I have listed some of the larger ones who are able to deliver further afield and some international organizations who may be able to offer advice on schemes in your area. Organic markets and farmers' markets offer an opportunity to buy produce that has been carefully raised on a small and sustainable scale. Discovering new sources of good quality produce is half the fun of eating organic – happy hunting!

CHEESE

Many supermarkets now stock a range of organic cheeses such as Cheddar and Brie but for more unusual varieties check out the mail order services listed below. These include both cheese-making farms and specialist shops:

CAERFAI CHEESES
St Davids, Wales
T. 01437 720 548
Make unpasteurized Cheddar, Caerphilly and Caerphilly with leeks and garlic.

THE CHEESE SHOP
Chester
T. 01244 346240
Sells a large range of organic traditionally-made farm cheese, including Staffordshire, Penbryn, Llangloffan, Pencarreg cheeses, Cornish herb, garlic and peppercorn, full-fat soft cow's milk cheese and Acorn organic ewe's milk cheese, plain or saffron coated.

IAIN MELLIS
Edinburgh and Glasgow
T. 0131 226 6215
They stock between 70 and 80 farm-made cheeses in their Scottish shops. Organic cheeses include Loch Arthur, Staffordshire and Orla Irish sheep's milk cheese.

LLANGLOFFAN FARMHOUSE
Haverfordwest, Wales
T: 01348 891 241
Their own cheese is a rich unpasteurized Cheshire-style cheese made from a mixture of Jersey and Brown Swiss cow's milk. Available plain, flavoured with chives and garlic and as a red Cheshire. Their farm shop also stocks other Welsh cheeses.

LOCH ARTHER
Dumfries, Scotland
T. 01387 760296
The creamery produces a range of organic unpasteurized hard and soft cheeses including an award-winning Cheddar, available plain or with herbs, a small soft cheese called Crannog and a semi-soft cheese called Criffel. They also sell a soft curd cheese and will make up mixed cheese platters and baskets for gifts.

NEAL'S YARD DAIRY
Covent Garden, London WC2
T: 020 7379 7646

Probably the biggest organic cheese store in the country and well worth a visit for any cheese lover. Organic cheeses include St Tola's goat's milk and Orla Irish sheep's milk cheese.

STAFFORDSHIRE ORGANIC
Newcastle-under-Lyme
T. 01782 680366
This cloth-bound unpasteurized Cheddar-style cheese is made both plain and flavoured with fresh herbs, dried herbs or wild garlic.

FISH

Pollution of the rivers and seas and the high use of pesticides in fish farming, means there is a need for organic accreditation for fish which comes from clean waters and organic fish farms. The following companies can provide these assurances – talk to them about the details.

GRAIG FARM
Powys, Wales
T. 01597 851655
This company import and sell wild fish, caught by dolphin-friendly hook and line in unpolluted waters off the island of St Helena in the Atlantic. This is the only Soil Association registered wild fish and is also 'fair-trade produce', with more of the price going to the islanders. The range includes: yellow fin tuna, albacore tuna, grouper, wahoo and mackerel. Graig Farm also sell farmed organic trout which comes from Cumbria.

THE ORKNEY SALMON COMPANY
Orkney
T. 01856 876101
The first certified organic fish farm which now supplies supermarkets.

SEVERN & WYE SMOKERY
Gloucestershire
T. 01452 750777
They sell fresh salmon from Glenarm and Clare Island organic fish farms, which are both located in Ireland. They also smoke the salmon in a traditional smokery. They are a good source of wild sea bass, but this is not certified organic.

SUMMER ISLES FOODS
Ross-shire, Scotland
T. 01854 622353
A traditional smokehouse in the far north-west Highlands of Scotland. They smoke salmon and other fish products which they first marinade in spiced brines with natural ingredients such as rum, molasses, juniper and garlic.

FLOUR

A wide range of organic, traditionally ground flour is available by mail order from the following small mills.

DOVES FARM
Berkshire
T. 01488 684880
Large range of stoneground flour and baked products, including spelt flour which is an ancient variety of wheat. Other products include Dove's Farm bread, biscuits and cornflakes – all organically certified.

LITTLE SALKELD WATERMILL
Penrith, Cumbria
T. 01768 881523
A traditional working water-powered mill offering a very wide range of flours and also wheat and rye grain for sprouting.

MAUD FOSTER MILL
Boston, Lincs.
T. 01205 352188
All their flours are milled from local organic grain and they produce unusual flours such as maize meal, pancake and chapati flours, together with their own muesli.

N.R.STOATE & SONS
Shaftesbury, Dorset
T. 01747 852475
A 19th-century waterwheel is the primary source of power that drives five pairs of French Burr Mill stones while a Portuguese windmill provides alternative power. Their wide range of flours are all stoneground and their organic flours are available as 100% wholemeal or plain brown.

PERRY COURT FARM
Chartham, Canterbury
T. 01227 738 8449
This is a Rudolf Steiner bio-dynamic farm which produces its own flour. It also has a farm shop and runs a vegetable box scheme.

SHIPTON MILL
Tetbury, Gloucestershire.
T. 01666 505050
A leading speciality bread flour miller whose flours are used by master bakers. They have recently introduced a gluten-free flour and a range of children's baking mixes to encourage children to bake. Their mail order service which is called Flour Direct, offers over twenty specialist flours and includes a contact number for personal bread-baking enquiries.

GROCERIES

You will increasingly find all you need in your local health food shops or supermarkets, but these people will supply general groceries by mail order:

ABEL & COLE
London
T. 0800 3764040

CERES NATURAL FOODS
Yeovil, Somerset
T. 01935 428791

COUNTRYSIDE WHOLEFOODS
London
T. 020 8363 2933

DAMHEAD ORGANICALLY GROWN FOODS
Edinburgh
T. 0131 445 1490

GREENCITY WHOLEFOODS
Glasgow
T. 0141 554 7633

LONGWOOD FARM
Suffolk
T. 01638 717120

ORGANIC HEALTH
Derbyshire
T. 01773 717718

MEAT AND POULTRY

GRAIG FARM
Powys, Wales
T. 01597 851655
Supplying a wide range of locally produced organic meat, they are the only source of organic mutton. They also produce hand-made pies and pizzas.

HARDWICK ESTATE
Reading
T. 0118 9842392
Beef, pork, lamb raised on the estate in the farm shop, The Old Dairy. Here they sell a wide range of organic products and in particular their own green top milk and cream.

HIGHER HACKNELL FARM
Umberleigh, Devon
T. 01769 560909
They supply their South Devon beef and lamb in large quantities and good prices, professionally butchered in a mixed box – all cuts included – for the freezer.

LONGWOOD FARM
Suffolk
T. 01638 717120
Longwood Farm specializes in sausages with the Suffolk, Pork & Herb and Pork & Apple being the favourites. They also rear and sell other meat, including Christmas geese and turkeys. They have stalls at three organic markets in London – Spitalfields on Sunday, Portobello on Thursday and Greenwich on Saturday. They also have a farm shop and an extensive mailing list featuring meat, dairy, fresh produce and bread.

MEAT MATTERS
Wantage, Oxfordshire
T. 01235 762461
Not only do Meat Matters operate an organic meat delivery service, they also deliver organic fruit and vegetable boxes.

NATURALLY YOURS
Ely, Cambridge
T 01353 778723
Offer a large range of meat, together with home-made sausages, cooked meat dishes and stir-fry packs.

ORGANIC AND FREE RANGE MEATS LTD
Fife, Scotland
T. 01738 850498
An organic farm since 1986, they produce their own meat and also sausages, bacon and haggis.

PURE MEAT DIRECT
Upper Stondon, Bedfordshire
T. 01462 851 5610
Their list of meats includes Eldon Wild Blue Pork, and stuffed meat is a speciality.

SWADDLES GREEN FARM
Somerset
T. 01460 234387
Offering a wide range of meat that has been raised on their own and on colleagues' land in the south west, Swaddles Green Farm also supplies an impressive range of ready-to-eat meals and general groceries.

ORGANIC FOODS LTD
Exeter, Devon
T. 01647 24724
This cooperative venture was set up by a group of organic producers. They can also supply vegetables on request.

SUNDRIES

HAMPERS HAMPERS
London
T. 020 8800 8008
This is a luxury hamper service, containing organic food, wine and chocolates.

THE VILLAGE BAKERY
Melmerby, Cumbria
T. 01768 881515
Bread, pastries, pies, puddings, jams and baking supplies.

PEPPERS BY POST
Dorchester, Dorset
T. 01308 897892
This venture was set up by chilli aficionados and they can supply an exciting range of home-grown fresh chilli peppers and aubergines unavailable anywhere else.

ANGLESEY SEA SALT CO.
Llanfairpwll, Wales
T. 01248 430871
Suppliers of organic sea salt.

HAMBLEDEN HERBS
Milverton, Somerset
T. 01823 401205

VEGETABLE BOX SCHEMES

These schemes have been phenomenally successful in Britain. They deliver vegetables and fruit fresh from the farm, important because organic produce is not sprayed with post-harvest preserving agents, so we need to receive it fast. The longer fruit and vegetables are on the shop shelves the more it will lose its health-giving vitamins. Many box schemes are operated by local people and this is important in establishing local food links. Larger schemes will also include dairy products, bread and a wide range of groceries. For a full list contact the Soil Association 0117 929 0661 or ask at your local health food store if they know of local organic farms or farmer's markets.

SCOTLAND

EAST COAST BOXES
East Lothian
T. 01875 340227

EPO GROWERS
Glasgow
T. 01398 875337

LENSHAW ORGANIC PRODUCE
Aberdeenshire
T.01464 871243

NORTH EAST ENGLAND

BRICKYARD FARM SHOP
Yorkshire
T. 01977 617327

FIELDGATE
Doncaster
T. 01302 846293

GOOSEMOORGANICS
Leeds
T. 01423 358887

NORTH EAST ORGANIC GROWERS
Northumberland
T. 01665 575785

NORTH WEST ENGLAND

GROWING WITH NATURE
Lancashire
T. 01253 421712

LIMITED RESOURCES
Manchester
T. 0161 226 4777

ORGANIC DIRECT
Liverpool
T. 0151 220 0220

RAMSBOTTOM VICTUALLERS
Ramsbottom
T. 01706 825070

NORTH WALES

DIMENSIONS
Gwynedd
T. 01248 351562

DISCOUNT ORGANICS
Flintshire
T. 01244 881209

SOUTH AND WEST WALES

PUMPKIN SHED
Pembrokeshire
T. 01437 721949

ROGERSWELL
Pembrokeshire
T. 01994 240237

WHITEBROOK ORGANIC GROWERS
Newport
T. 01633 689253

WELSH BORDERS

ABUNDANCE PRODUCE
Herefordshire
T. 01981 540181

GREENLINK ORGANIC FOODS
Worcestershire
T. 01531 640140

SHROPSHIRE HILLS ORGANIC PRODUCE
Shropshire
T. 01588 60735

MIDLANDS

CHEVELSWARDE ORGANIC GROWERS
Leicestershire
T. 01858 575309

NATURAL DELIVERY WHOLEFOODS
Derbyshire
T. 01433 620383

ORGANIC ROUNDABOUT
Birmingham
T. 0121 551 1679

ORGANIC TRAIL
Buckinghamshire
T. 01908 614747

THE ORGANIC WHOLEFOOD NETWORK
Hertfordshire
T. 01923 490526

EAST OF ENGLAND

BLYTON ORGANICS
Lincolnshire
T. 01427 628928

DJ PRODUCE
Suffolk
T. 01638 552709

GREENS ORGANIC FOODS
Norfolk
T. 01379 890199

NATURALLY YOURS
Cambridgeshire
T. 01353 778723

ORGANIC CONNECTIONS INTERNATIONAL
Cambridgeshire
T. 01945 773374

WHEELBARROW FOODS
North Lincolnshire
T. 01469 530721

WOLDS ORGANIC FOODS
Lincolnshire
T. 01507 610686

GREATER LONDON

ABEL & COLE
London
T. 0800 376 4040

FARM-A-ROUND
London
T. 020 8291 3650

THE FRESH FOOD COMPANY
London
T. 020 8969 0351

ORGANICS DIRECT
London
T. 020 7729 2828

SOUTH-EAST ENGLAND

ASHURST ORGANICS
E. Sussex
T. 01273 891219

BARCOMBE NURSERIES
E. Sussex
T. 01273 400011

DABBS PLACE ORGANIC FARM
Kent
T. 01474 814333

HARVEST SUPPLIES
E. Sussex
T. 01342 823392

RIPPLE FARM
Kent
T. 01227 730898

SURREY ORGANICS
Surrey
T. 01483 300424

SOUTHERN ENGLAND

GODSHILL ORGANICS
Isle of Wight
T. 01983 840723

NORTHDOWN ORCHARD
Hampshire
T. 01256 771477

ORGANIC LIFE
Berkshire
T. 01628 639054

WEST OF ENGLAND

ARCADIA ORGANICS
Somerset
T. 01934 876886

THE BETTER FOOD COMPANY
Bristol
T. 01275 474545

SLIPSTREAM ORGANICS
Gloucestershire
T. 01242 227273

SOUTH-WEST OF ENGLAND

DARTMOOR DIRECT
Devon
T. 01364 651528

HIGHFIELD FARM SHOP
Devon
T. 01392 876388

RIVERFORD ORGANIC VEGETABLES
Devon
T. 01803 762720

TREGANNICK FARM
Cornwall
T. 01822 833969

ORGANIC MARKETS & FARMER'S MARKETS

For information about when and where these markets are held, contact the Soil Association (see page 188).

WINE AND BEER

AVALON VINEYARD
Somerset
T. 01749 860393
Produces organic wines, cider and fruit wines from their own fruit. By mail order by the case (of no less than ten bottles), plus delivery charge.

CHUDLEIGH VINEYARD
Devon
T. 01626 8533 248
Produces four white wines which are available by the case, including delivery.

DUNKERTON CIDER
Herefordshire
T. 01544 388653
Produces a variety of ciders and perrys available by the case, including delivery.

SEDDLESCOMBE VINEYARD
East Sussex
T. 01580 830715
Produces white wines, cider and apple and pear juice. Mail order catalogue available.

VINCEREMOS WINES AND SPIRITS
Leeds
T. 0113 257 7545
Vinceremos@aol.com
Specialist wine merchant selling a large range of wines, spirits, beers and juices. Mail order catalogue available.

VINTAGE ROOTS
Berkshire
T. 0118 940 1222
Stockists of the largest range of organic wines available in the country. They also supply organic mead and ginger wine together with beers, ciders and fruit juices. Mail order catalogue available.

ORGANIC CERTIFICATION BODIES

Throughout the world there are organizations which monitor and certify organic farmers and growers. Some of these are members of IFOAM (International Federation of Organic Agriculture Movement) and some are regulated by the European Community.

ARGENTINA

ARGENCERT (IFOAM)
Bernardo de Irioyen 760,
17D (1072) Buenos Aires
T. 54 1 334 2943
F. 54 1 331 7185
argencert@interlink.co.ar

AUSTRALIA

NATIONAL ASSOCIATION OF SUSTAINABLE AGRICULTURE AUSTRALIA (NASAA)
PO Box 768, Stirling 5152,
South Australia
T. 61 88 3708455
F. 61 88 3708381

AUSTRIA

SGS, AUSTRIA CONTROLL & CO GES. M.B.H
Johannesgasse 14
A-1010 Wien

BELGIUM

ECOCERT BELGIUM SPRL/BVBA
Av. de l'Escrime 85 Schermlaan
B-1150 Bruxelles - Brussel
T. 32.10.81.44.94
F. 32.10.81.42.50

BOLIVIA

BOLICERT (IFOAM)
Casilla 13030,
General Gonzales 1317, La Paz
T. & F. 591 2 310846

BRAZIL

INSTITUTO BIODINAMICO (IFOAM)
Caixa Postal 321,
CEP 18603-970 Botucatu SP
T. 55 149 75 9011
F. 55 148 22 5066

FINLAND

NATIONAL FOOD ADMINISTRATION
P.O.Box 111
FIN - 32201 LOIMAA
T. 358-2-760561
F. 358-9-7726 7666

FRANCE

ECOCERT S.A.R.L
B.P. 47
32600 L'Isle Jourdain
T. 33-5-62-07 34 24

GERMANY

NATURLAND-VERBAND (IFOAM)
Kleinhaderner Weg 1, 82166
Grafelfing
T. 49 89 8545071
F. 49 89 855974
Naturland.Germany@t-online.de

GREECE

ASSOCIATION OF ECOLOGICAL AGRICULTURE OF GREECE (SOYE)
26, Averof Str, GR - 10433 Athens
T. 01-8234826

HOLLAND

SKAL
Stationsplein 5, Postbus 384,
8000 AJ ZWOLLE
T. 31/38.42.68181
F. 31/38.42.13.063

ICELAND

VISTFRAEDISTOFAN
Lifraen Islensk Vottun, Saevarhofda
4, 112 Reykjavik

IRELAND

IRISH ORGANIC FARMERS AND GROWERS ASSOC.
56 Blessington Street, Dublin 7
T. 00 353 18307996
F. 00 353 18300925

ITALY

BIOAGRICOOP SCRL (IFOAM)
Via Fucini 10, 10-40033,
Caselecchio di Reno (BO)
T. 39 0 51 6130512
F. 39 0 51 6130224
bioagric@iperbole.bologna.it

LUXEMBOURG

ADMINISTRATION DES SERVICE TECHNIQUES DE L'AGRICULTURE
PO Box 1904, L-1019 Luxembourg

NEW ZEALAND

BIO-GRO NEW ZEALAND (IFOAM)
PO Box 9693 Marion Square,
Wellington 6031
T. 64 4 801 9741
F. 64 4 801 9742
levick@bio-gro.co.nz

NORWAY

NORWEGIAN AGRICULTURAL INSPECTION SERVICE
Post-box 3, 1430

PORTUGAL

SOCERT-PORTUGAL CERTIFICACAO ECOLOGICA, LDA
Rua Joao de Matos Bilhau,
No 11 loja 13, 2520 Peniche
T. 062-785117
F. 062-785117

SPAIN

DIRECCION GENERAL DE COMERCIALIZACION E INDUSTRIALIZACION AGROALIMENTARIA
Consejeria de Agricultura y Medio Ambiente, c/Pintor Matias Moreno, 4, 45002 Toledo
T. 925-266 750
F. 925-266 722

SWEDEN

KRAV (IFOAM)
Box 1940, S-751 49 Uppsala
T. 46 181 00290
F. 46 181 00366
eva.mattsson@krav.se

UNITED KINGDOM

SOIL ASSOCIATION CERTIFICATION LTD (IFOAM)
Bristol House, 40-56 Victoria Street, Bristol, BS1 6BY
T. 0117 929 0661/914 2400
F. 0117 925 2504
soilassoc@gn.apc.org

UKROFS (THE UNITED KINGDOM REGISTER OF ORGANIC FOOD STANDARDS)
c/o Ministry of Agriculture Fisheries and Food,
Room G 43, Nobel House,
17 Smith Square, London,
SW1P 3JR
T. 020 7238 5915
F. 020 7238 6148

ORGANIC FARMERS AND GROWERS
50 High Street, Soham, Ely,
Cambridgeshire, CB7 5HF
T. 01353 722398

BIODYNAMIC AGRICULTURAL ASSOCIATION
The Painswick Inn Project,
Gloucester Street, Stroud
GL5 1QG
T. 01453 759501
F. 01453 759501

UNITED STATES

CALIFORNIA CERTIFIED ORGANIC FARMERS (IFOAM)
1115 Mission Street, Santa Cruz,
CA 95060
T. 1 408 423 2263
F. 1 408 423 4528
dianeb@ccof.org

OREGON TILTH (IFOAM)
1860 Hawthorne NE, Suite 200,
Salen, Oregon 97303
T. 1 503 378 0690
F. 1 503 378 0809
organic@tilth.org

ORGANIC GROWERS AND BUYERS ASSOCIATION (OGBA) (IFOAM)
8525 Edinbrook Crossing, Suite 3,
Brooklyn Park, MN 55443
T. 1 612 424 2450
F. 1 612 315 2733
ogba@sprynet.com

USEFUL ADDRESSES

ENVIRONMENT AND HEALTH NEWS
PO Box 1954, Glastonbury,
Somerset BA6 9FE
T. 01603 765670

THE FOOD MAGAZINE
The Food Commission (UK) Ltd,
5-11 Worship Street, London
EC2A 2BH
T. 020 7628 7774

FRIENDS OF THE EARTH
26 Underwood Street,
London N1
T. 020 7490 1555

GREENPEACE
Canonbury Villas, London
N1 2PN
T. 020 7865 8100

THE HENRY DOUBLEDAY RESEARCH ASSOCIATION
Ryton Organic Gardens,
Ryton-on-Dunsmore, Coventry,
CV8 3LG
T. 024 76303517

INTERNATIONAL FEDERATION OF ORGANIC AGRICULTURAL MOVEMENTS
Okozentrum Imsbach,
D-66636, Tholey-Theley, Germany
T. 49 6853 5190

THE SOIL ASSOCIATION
Bristol House, 40-56 Victoria
Street, Bristol BS1 6BY
T. 0117 929 0661
F. 0117 925 2504

WOMAN'S ENVIRONMENTAL NETWORK
87 Worship Street, London
EC2A 2BE
T. 020 7247 3327
www.gn.apc.org/wen

FURTHER READING

E For Additives
Maurice Hanssen, Thorsons, 1987

Environment and Health News
Available from PO Box 1954,
Glastonbury, Somerset BA6 9FE
T. 01603 765670

The Food Magazine
Available from The Food
Commission (UK) Ltd,
5-11 Worship Street, London
EC2A 2BH
T. 020 7628 7774

The Food We Eat
Joanna Blythman, Penguin, 1996
Go Organic Magazine
Available from 27 Bell Street,
Reigate, Surrey, RH2 7AD

Healthy Eating for Babies & Children
Food Commission, Hodder &
Stoughton, 1995

Organic Café Cookbook
Carol Charlton, David & Charles,
1999

The Organic Directory
Available from Clive Litchfield,
Green Earth Books, Foxhole,
Dartington, Totnes, Devon
TQ9 6EB
T. 01803 863260

The Shoppers Guide to Organic Food
Linda Brown, Fourth Estate,
1998

The Silent Spring
Rachel Carson, Penguin, 1999 (new
edition)

What the Doctors Don't Tell You
Available from 4 Wallace Road,
London N1 2PG
T. 020 7354 4592

Where to Buy Organic
Available from The Soil Association
Bristol House, 40-56 Victoria
Street, Bristol, BS1 6BY
T. 0117 9290661
F. 0117 9252504